DAVE STOVALL

Foreword by Alisa Childers

LOSING
MY
FAITH

in Progressive Christianity

a renew.org discipling resource

Losing My Faith is such a timely book for those who once walked the narrow path and then became disillusioned. Dave's journey shines a light on the hope that is found only in God's grace and mercy.

—**TobyMac**, Grammy Award-winning artist, producer, and songwriter

I've been a fan of Dave's music, his lyrics, and his genius for many years…and this book reminds me of why. Dave is not just a gifted storyteller and composer; he relentlessly chases Truth. This beautiful and candid story of Dave re-constructing his faith couldn't be timelier for this generation. Well done, Dave!

—**Mark Stuart**, two-time Grammy Award winner, lead singer of Audio Adrenaline

Dave tells his story from childhood church experience to deconstruction and then to reestablishing his faith. He transparently shares his experiences while giving insight into what leads so many down a similar path of doubt and struggle. I'll share this book with those I disciple as a poignant look at what can happen when we choose feelings over truth and how to love people back to the beauty of the saving gospel in Christ Jesus.

—**Michelle Eagle**, Discipleship and Women's Minister, Harpeth Christian Church, co-author of *Identity: Who You Really Are in Christ*

Dave's journey out of deconstruction/progressive Christianity is a story I'm passionate about. His journey back to Truth is something we should champion, and I pray it helps others who have drifted into the cultural norms of Christianity instead of what authentic Christianity really is. The voices of those who are promoting deconstruction are loud, and I'm proud to stand behind Dave as a voice in culture of combating compromise with truth and love!

—**Seth Morrison**, guitarist of Skillet

Dave Stovall brings an honest, open, and real conversation to the idea of faith—that it needs to be our own as a sincere seeking and ultimately finding what real relationship with the one true God looks like. It's the search of the ages, and as we ask, seek, and knock, the door will be open to us. Thank you, Dave, for such a heartfelt journey which inspires us all.

—**Will McGinniss**, Audio Adrenaline and Hands and Feet Project

Dave Stovall is my co-worker and the worship leader at our church. This is a life-changing book, written by a man who is thoughtful and who is the real deal, dealing with the real issues today.

—**Bobby Harrington**, Point Leader, Renew.org and Discipleship.org

For
All who wander
But are not lost

CONTENTS

FOREWORD

There once was a fifteen-year-old son of an army chaplain who was sent to a Christian boarding school. While at the institution, he began to encounter deep and agonizing doubts about Christianity. When he asked his teachers to answer his questions and give logical reasons for their beliefs, they weren't able to…at least to his satisfaction. He finally wrote a letter to his father in which he confessed that he no longer believed Jesus to be divine, the cross to be substitutionary, or hell to be an eternal place of punishment. The year was 1787, and his name was Friedrich Schleiermacher.

If this were to happen today, Schleiermacher might jump on social media to announce his deconstruction. He might celebrate his much more tolerant and inclusive way of approaching Christianity by sweeping harmful beliefs like vicarious atonement, the deity of Jesus, and the doctrine of hell out of the way. Of course, in Schleiermacher's day, the technology necessary to do such a thing did not yet exist. Instead, he went on to become a hospital chaplain and professor of theology and religion and is remembered today as the Father of Theological Liberalism.

Theological Liberalism—which approaches the Bible as a book more human than divine—swept through the church, splitting many denominations in two. This is why today denominations like the Presbyterian church is divided into the more liberal PCUSA and the more conservative PCA. The mainline churches represent liberal theology, while the Evangelical churches represent conservative theology, which seeks to conserve the historic doctrines of the faith. Over the course of the last hundred years or so, liberal theology has caused the mainline denominations to go into decline. Yet at the same time, liberal theology is alive and well and seeming to flourish even in Evangelical churches. Why is this?

In my estimation, theological liberalism is a bit like a parasite that attaches to its host unnoticed. It feeds on it, making it weak and sick. This particular parasite ate its way through the liberal denominations and is now looking for a new host. That new host? The Evangelical church. However, it's no longer referred to as Theological Liberalism, but as something that sounds a lot more positive and enlightened. It's called Progressive Christianity now, and it's sweeping through the church. Due to the accessibility of social media and the proliferation of books, podcasts, blogs, and YouTube channels by self-professed progressive Christians, it has fully invaded many Evangelical churches. We now find ourselves at a similar crossroads as Schleiermacher in the 18th century. Will we stand on the eternal truths of God's Word, or will we adapt Christianity to our times?

Like Dave, I recorded music and toured as a part of the contemporary Christian music industry. It's a tough business. Sadly, there isn't much accountability or doctrinal standards. As a recording artist, my life was a constant cycle of touring, writing, recording, and then more touring, writing, and recording. There wasn't much down time, and I quickly became physically and spiritually exhausted and depleted.

After my time in CCM was over, my husband and I put down roots in a local church. There was a sense of excitement as this church was growing exponentially due to the young, eloquent, and charismatic pastor. A brilliant orator, he brought insights into the Scriptures I'd never heard before. After a while, I was invited to a small study group facilitated by the pastor that he compared to a seminary education. Yet I was totally unprepared for many of the core beliefs I'd held about God, Jesus, and the Bible to be deconstructed and explained away. It propelled me into my own faith crisis that took me years to recover from. Years later, this church would rebrand itself as a "progressive Christian community." I watched many of my friends deconstruct into progressive Christianity. Most have not found their way back.

This is why Dave Stovall's story of deconstructing into progressive Christianity only to be discipled back to the historic faith is so breathtakingly inspiring. It's a story you don't often hear. *Losing My Faith…in Progressive Christianity* is an important book because it demonstrates that there is hope. Dave did the excruciatingly hard work of studying the Bible in context. Even as a progressive Christian, he was open-minded enough to allow his pastor to question some of his assumptions. He was teachable enough to doubts his doubts. He was curious enough to allow the Word of God challenge his preconceived conclusions. What he found was a God that is way bigger than progressive Christianity can fathom.

HE WAS TEACHABLE ENOUGH TO DOUBTS HIS DOUBTS.

In a culture where deconstruction stories are now the norm, this book was the shot of encouragement I needed. I pray that Dave's story is the first of many. After all, the beauty of the orthodox Christian faith is vibrant, robust, and satisfying. It answers the deepest questions of life. I pray that many more progressive Christians would follow Dave's example and discover something Schleiermacher lost: the beauty of the true gospel.

As G. K. Chesterton put it (and with my addition): "It is easy to be a heretic. It is always easy to let the age have its head; the difficult thing is to keep one's own. It is always easy to be a modernist; as it is easy to be a snob. To have fallen into any one of the fads from Gnosticism to Christian Science [to progressive Christianity] would indeed have been obvious and tame. But to have avoided them all has been one whirling adventure; and in my vision the heavenly chariot flies thundering through the ages, the dull heresies sprawling and prostrate, the wild truth reeling but erect."

—Alisa Childers, author of *Another Gospel* and *The Deconstruction of Christianity*

INTRODUCTION

You know what I hate? Book introductions that ruin the ending of a good book. Like…why would anyone ever do that? I read a book once that did that, and I got so mad I had a hard time actually finishing the book. I tried my hardest to flick my eyes away while simultaneously picking out the words "when…he… dies…at…the…end" and then let out a frustrated, "You've got to be kidding me." Don't worry. I'm not going to spoil the ending here. I think I've pretty much already done that with the title.

I also hate long introductions almost as much as the ones that ruin the ending, so let's get down to business. I am so thankful you have a copy of this book. It's my first ever, official book and I'm excited to see how the Lord will use it. I was getting tired of seeing a lot of my friends (some from the Christian music industry I was in) go public in really artsy, catchy ways with sharing their deconstruction stories. Their narratives moved me for a while, but then God began moving me back toward him.

I began to wonder if there were any other people like me that wandered from the Christian faith but didn't end up becoming agnostic or atheist. So, I started writing. And (more scarily) I started sharing publicly. I began to realize I wasn't alone, and that lots of people have experienced the same thing as I—being a Christian who simply wasn't sure for a while. And I've learned that some of those people were wrestling with the same things during the exact time frame that I was experiencing this strange season of my life.

Doubting the faith you've held so close all your life really sucks. It's an awful feeling that I wouldn't wish on anyone. But doubt sort of just springs up on you and you gotta deal with it, otherwise it can consume you. I've since learned that while I was seemingly suffering alone, there were countless other believers suffering alone right next to me. Hearing others' similar experiences in the darkness of doubt helps me to know that what God did for me on the other side was real, and it's helped me understand what he is continuing to do through our questions and rigorous honesty with each other.

Have you had serious doubts or questions about God or your salvation, or do you know someone who has? Have you ever sat in a church service full of excited Christians on fire for the Lord and wondered, "What's wrong with me? Why am I not like that? Am I not truly saved?" If so, then this book is for you. By the end of it, you won't feel alone anymore, and I hope I'll do a good job of normalizing the ups and downs on the path for every true believer.

It's okay to go through seasons of doubt and seasons of certainty. Those are both signs that your faith is real. No one who follows Christ always enjoys a smooth-sailing experience. If they do, I'm not sure if they're really following Jesus or just going to church while calling their own shots and living comfortably. The ride with the Holy Spirit is bumpy. Turbulence is to be

IT'S OKAY TO GO THROUGH SEASONS OF DOUBT AND SEASONS OF CERTAINTY.

expected. Doubts and questions should be interpreted as clear signs that faith is real, not that it's lacking. If things in the Bible aren't making you think deeply, if they aren't challenging you, then they may not be going down far enough to actually touch your heart. And that's a scarier scenario than wrestling with a bout of the doubt.

On the flip side, are you good right where you are? Are you sitting comfortably in a faith that remains unchallenged? Do you want to avoid going down the rabbit hole of understanding why you question your faith or why people deconstruct and walk away? Are you content to avoid diving deeper into the knowledge of God by swimming blissfully on the surface of the lake? If so, don't read any further. This isn't the book for you. Go check out a Joel Osteen book or something.

But if you want to understand what it looks like to wade through the waters of wonder and step into the upside-down world of examining your faith...I'll see you in chapter 1.

1
FIRM FOUNDATION?

"Welcome, in the Lion's name. Come further up
and further in."
—C. S. Lewis, *The Last Battle*

I grew up in the South. When I say *South*, I mean population
of 3,000, 97% white, Southern Baptist, praise-God-and-bless-
America, evangelical-as-it-gets Alabama. In that bubble I was
completely happy. Just about everyone in my family was a
Christian, so from an early age I knew I wanted to be one, too.
At eight years old, I walked down the aisle, and the preacher told
me how to say a prayer and ask Jesus into my heart. I got baptized
two weeks later.

This happened during the glorious 1990s. There was a little
thing in Southern church culture called The Sinner's Prayer. Every
preacher preached it, and every good Christian kid walked down
an aisle and said it and hopefully meant it the right way (or they

might just be eternally damned to hell. No pressure on getting this right…). My preacher said this was the way to salvation, the revival guest preachers said it, freaking Billy Graham said it, so I just took it as truth.

No one told me the Sinner's Prayer was actually a relatively recent trend. Some would say it was invented as early as the 18th century revival movements and kicked into high gear (especially in children's ministries) in the 1970s. "All you gotta do is ask Jesus into your heart," they would say. The prayer went something like this: "God, I admit that I'm a sinner. I believe that Jesus died on the cross for me. I confess that Jesus is Lord. Please come into my heart and save me. Amen."

Very simple. It's not hard to see why that caught on so well. I mention this now because, eventually, I had trouble squaring the simplicity and assurance of the Sinner's Prayer with my recurring doubts. This confusion became one of the first cracks in the southern Christian tradition I was handed as a young boy that then led me down a series of more cracks and eventually to a deconstruction of my faith.

More on that later. For now, let's jump back into that glorious decade: the 90s. After becoming a Christian, I grew up to become a JNCO jeans-wearing spiritual leader in the youth group in my teens. Sure, I had questions about aliens, but never about God. Somehow, he was off limits in my mind and questioning him *out loud* was definitely off limits. These years were the easy times in my faith.

But in junior college, a crack would form in that previously firm foundation.

A GROWING SENSE OF DOUBT

I was heavily involved in the Baptist Student Union on my college campus. It was basically a ministry to keep students on the "straight and narrow." I was the praise and worship team leader, went on all the street witnessing trips, and eventually became the president of the Baptist Student Union.

But then something happened. There was a spot behind the girls' dorm, an empty parking lot, where I would go to pray. Bear with me; that sounds creepier than it actually was. I would go out there to the empty parking lot, look up at the sky, and enjoy the feeling of the presence of God.

One day I drove out there and did all the same things I **ONE GIANT THING WAS MISSING: GOD.** had been doing, but one giant thing was missing: God.

I looked to the sky and felt this horrible self-realizing feeling go through my bones. It was the feeling of being totally alive and yet utterly alone. I was so confused. I tried to pray but I couldn't feel God's presence or his love like I had before.

It is important to note here that I wasn't living in any ongoing, unrepentant sin. Sometimes God removes his presence from people, and unrepentant sin is definitely a reason for that, but that wasn't the case for me. I wasn't sinless by any means, but I was regularly confessing and repenting whenever I did stumble into sin.

So, I eventually just drove back to my dorm room wondering how I was going to hide from my roommate (also a leader at the BSU) the fact that I wasn't sure if God was real. I waited weeks for the fear to pass, but it didn't. In fact, the crack only widened and deepened. Had Jesus just been an imaginary friend this whole time? How could I know I was really saved? Did I do it right when I was eight years old? Did it stick? Now, every sermon I heard, every person I talked to that seemed confident in their faith actually scared me. I felt fake—like everyone thought I was like them, but inside I was different.

Finally, I got up the courage to tell someone.

I told my best friend that I was doubting if God existed and I wasn't sure if I was a real Christian. He encouraged me and reminded me of Romans 10:9: "If you declare with your mouth, 'Jesus is Lord,' and believe in your heart that God raised him from the dead, you *will* be saved." But then he warned me that if I ever felt that way again, I should probably get saved…again.

I nodded in agreement, but I could feel a cold sweat. I knew I would feel it again. In fact, I was already feeling it again in that moment. I started declaring "Jesus is Lord" pretty often in my prayers. I said it to the Lord but also to myself, as a means of telling myself, *"Wake up, soul, and believe this again!"* Yet the feeling remained. I started to wonder how saying a phrase or a prayer could actually save me and keep me from the flames of hell.

Remember that Sinner's Prayer I told you about? Well, at this point, I'm basically saying that prayer every few hours of every day, hoping to God it worked that time.

What a miserable existence. Interestingly though, as I look back, I never read anywhere in the Bible that I was supposed to "ask Jesus into my heart." Nowhere. You'd think that would've been a huge red flag for me, but at the time it wasn't. I just believed whatever I had been told.

So, there I was, the leader of a Christian ministry, yet losing my faith completely. I reached out to another friend. I was vulnerable with him about my doubts. His response was literally to shame me. He said, "Salvation is the core of our religion; if you're doubting that...then something is really wrong with you."

Gee, thanks for the help. Like I needed to be reminded of that.

If I wasn't sure I should keep these doubts and questions to myself before that Jesus-juke, then I was definitely sure afterward.

The funny thing about the timing of the doubts is that, before all this happened, I had agreed to be a summer missionary after that semester ended. So, I wrapped up my sophomore year and headed to the "but it's a dry heat" state of Arizona, where I began serving churches out there. The doubts remained, but being out there with no one I really knew was a huge learning experience for me. I started scratching the surface of what God was aiming to do with me. And what was that? He was going to teach me a very valuable lesson that would not only carry me through difficult times in my faith, but also through hard times in marriage and the letdowns of my career: God wanted to show me how to walk through life without leaning on feelings alone but trusting in his words. Instead of rushing to chase feelings of anxiety away with momentary feelings of relief through "praying the prayer," I would eventually learn to let the feelings be there while I refocused my trust on *him*, not on a particular internal mood.

Learning that lesson has carried me through every major step in life. I had to walk through a dark night of the soul and believe that, even though I may have felt blindfolded, I was still in the light. That was a hard thing to do. At times it felt like lying to myself. But I knew deep down that God was there and that I wasn't crazy. I believe all faithful Christians at some point will need to learn how to love and trust God even when we don't feel like he's there.

After surviving the dry heat that summer, I returned to college with a refreshed faith that was stronger than before. But one thing was different for sure: I had a new distrust for things I had learned in my Bible-belt upbringing.

I HAD A NEW DISTRUST FOR THINGS I HAD LEARNED IN MY BIBLE-BELT UPBRINGING.

The lack of explanation and understanding for the season of doubt I had just been through, mixed with the whole Sinner's Prayer business, made me feel like an outsider; like I wasn't like the "them" I knew in conservative church circles.

The anxiety began shifting into arrogance. In my mind, they didn't understand what it meant to wrestle with God. Rather, they seemed to look down on the struggle as wrong and a lack of true faith. They didn't seem to wonder about things like how a "magical" prayer could save a soul. They didn't seem interested in looking deeper. Somehow, they seemed simpler than where I was headed mentally. And to be honest, I didn't really want to be a part of what they were doing anymore. Before, I felt like I was the fake Christian; now it felt more like the opposite. It looked to me like I was the one following Christ, while they were following a system of traditions made up by man. So, I decided I was going to find out more about the cultural Christian traditions I was handed. I wanted to know where those beliefs came from. I wanted to inspect the roots.

And so began my journey away from the faith and back again.

QUESTIONS FOR DISCUSSION AND REFLECTION

1. Many of us have childhood church traditions. Describe one that you think or know isn't in the Bible?
2. What is a question that you have about God that you are afraid to ask?
3. Describe a season of doubt you've had in your life.
4. Dave's vulnerability was met with casting shame. What would have been a more helpful response?
5. Read Jude 1:22. How can you apply this verse in your life?

6. How does Dave's experience mirror your own or that of someone you know?

2
NOTHING LIKE
THESE PEOPLE

So there I was, a young college student figuring out life and sitting in my old home church watching *Left Behind*. I'm not exactly sure how I ended up there or on the front row, but alas, there I was. My church planned a whole night around this movie. We were Baptists, so of course there was a potluck including about seven different kinds of mac 'n' cheese (all of them fantastic).

I watched the movie with everyone and honestly tried to keep from physically cringing. It wasn't just the mediocre acting (sorry if you like these movies) or production (my distaste for bad art with the Christian label on it could be its own separate chapter). It was the theology in it and the growing feeling that I was the only one in the church gymnasium that night who thought the Bible didn't clearly teach the theology that the book and movie series were based on.

I knew the people around me were taking in the story as a literal look at how the end would happen. I felt sick. I bet I was visibly sweating. People probably thought it was just the potluck sweats, but it was my thinking that I wasn't like "these people"—these "simple-minded people." It makes me sad now to say that I even had those thoughts, but I really did.

I wondered if anyone else cared to know if there was more to this faith than what our preacher was telling us.

I wanted to know if the Christians in this church had any idea that this spiritual "pool" we were swimming in had a deep end. Or if they cared to know if the depths of knowledge and wisdom of God that would satisfy our souls as well as our intellects could be found? Did the average Christian even have an intellect that needed satisfying? At the time, I really didn't think so. But I knew by this point that I did.

> **DID THE AVERAGE CHRISTIAN EVEN HAVE AN INTELLECT THAT NEEDED SATISFYING?**

In chapter 1, I said some harsh things about my old home church and also in the paragraph before this one. But you know what? My first church was also where my love for God began to grow. It was where I made my first friends. I had a ton of fun growing up there. We spent real time together back then. The leadership put on silly plays and costume parties and all sorts of things seemingly just to be together.

All of that worked with me up to a certain point (or age), and then it just wasn't enough.

The reason I mention this is that I really want you to see and understand how I went from feeling, "I'm one of you" to, "Something's wrong with me, can you help?" to, "I am nothing like you; in fact, I'm actually way smarter than you."

So, before I attended this potluck and *Left Behind* night, I had been trying to find the theology or traditions that had worked their way into the church like bad yeast. Well, the first one I found, almost by accident, was the premillennial dispensationalist view of the end times. That's fancy talk for the *Left Behind* view of the end or, as I like to refer to it, the Kirk Cameron Eschatology.

THREE BUCKETS

I want to explain something that will hopefully make this next section as unoffensive as it can be. The last thing I want to do is offend anyone's personal beliefs. I learned from my current church to put biblical truths in three buckets to help with disagreements within our religion, and I've found these three categories super helpful for peaceful conversations.

Essential truths. Things essential to our salvation. This includes beliefs like Jesus being the Son of God, the fact that Jesus literally died and literally rose again. Stuff like that. By all means, let's try to persuade people on these points.

Important truths. This bucket encompasses issues in the Bible where you will find a range of beliefs, but all still fall under the umbrella of Christianity, meaning we can still behave like family even when disagreeing over these issues. They are *important* for living a faithful life but are not essentials for one's salvation. These views will affect how you live out your faith, but disagreeing on them doesn't fundamentally determine your eternal stance with God.

Personal beliefs. This would include things like alcohol, secular music, rated-R movies, and—in my opinion—your eschatology (particular beliefs about how the end times will unfold). Because of grey area and/or silence on these issues in the Bible, these things are left up to the believer and their conscience before the Lord in deciding if they will do or believe these things.

In my experience, as I'm sure you can probably relate, people tend to get hung up over arguing about personal bucket things and end up wasting each other's time and giving Christians a bad rap with the watching world.

RAPTURE THEOLOGY

Because there is a lot of ambiguity in Scripture about the end times, and end-times theories which hinge on some gray-area verses, I believe our differing views on, for example, the "Rapture," the "Tribulation," and the "Millennium" are actually personal-bucket beliefs. Your belief on these doesn't determine whether you are a true follower of Christ. A person's end times beliefs aren't good reason to get in a theological fight or to make judgments about a person's salvation. And hiding behind, "Well, I just *like* to talk about these things" all the while pulling people into heated discussions still counts as a theological fight (yeah, I see you).

That being said, my personal belief is that the view that all Christians will be raptured off the face of the planet before things get really bad just isn't the most accurate way to interpret the verses about the end. That doesn't mean you're wrong and I'm right. But because I was taught very strongly that this view was the *only* right view for *real* Christians, it caused another crack in my foundation when I couldn't find clear evidence in Scripture to support the idea.

I was confused as I read through Revelation for the first time by myself and didn't find a single reference to a rapture. I was actually blown away. I thought surely it would be in the book about the end, but it wasn't in there—much like the Sinner's Prayer. All I could find was a reference in 1 Thessalonians about meeting Jesus in the air, along with the believers who have died before us, to be with him forever. Again, I started to wonder how much of this stuff was just decided on by some high-up leader and taught to the masses with confidence. I was totally freaked out. I once was unquestioningly secure in my faith and now I could only see the flaws.

NOW I COULD ONLY SEE THE FLAWS.

The church used to be a beautiful and pure thing in my mind. Now it was becoming something like a facade covering up a giant pyramid scheme.

I'm hoping by now you're seeing the trend. The questioning, the unrest, the wondering how no one else feels or thinks this way, and the eventual landing place of thinking I'm better than these simple-minded…Christians. It's pretty easy now to see the spiritual car wreck I was heading toward, but at the time it was impossible for me to see, behind the wheel speeding around the curve. People even tried to warn me, but it wouldn't stop me. By this point I had made up my mind that I wasn't going to be defined by the word "evangelical" anymore.

That word had come to mean something different to me. It didn't mean traditional Protestant Christian who affirms the authority and historicity of the Bible. It meant Bible-thumping, Republican, gay-hating, straight-laced, no fun, judgmental, K-LOVE listening, borderline-prosperity-gospel hypocrite. Truthfully, those were the kind of Christians I was surrounded by.

WHAT WOULD HAVE HELPED

It would have helped if I had met a genuine person during this time who said, "Hey, I get it. Sometimes this stuff is hard to believe. Some days I have doubts and questions. Other days, I'm on fire for the Lord. That's just kind of how it goes. Mountains and valleys. But when you're His, He is with you through it all."

That's what I would say to my twenty-something-year-old, doubting self. "Hang in there, kid. This too shall pass."

It did pass. But before it did, I had a lot of ground to cover because I had been burned when being open about this stuff. I pretty much faced it alone...until I started a band with four of my best friends and started touring the country.

We called ourselves *Freshmen15* after the weight we all put on during our first year in college. We were a pop-punk Christian band on fire for the Lord and we had two missions:

1. To show the world that following Christ wasn't boring (you could be fun and be a Christian), and
2. To *not* be disingenuous like the other cookie-cutter Christian bands we had played with.

So, we bought an old church van (well, my super supportive parents did), and we hit the road. What an amazing time. One of the perks was getting to meet different Christians from all over the country. Our Southern culture looked a lot different from the West Coast and even the Christian culture in Nashville. It was in Nashville where we met the first person who genuinely loved God, cared about people, *but also* drank alcohol—*gasp!*—and even sometimes *cussed (BIGGER GASP!).* In the next chapter, I'll expound upon the three well-known unforgivable sins—drinking, smoking, and cussing. For now, I'd like to end this chapter with a word of encouragement if you've felt a resonance with my story so far.

A QUICK SIDE NOTE AND ENCOURAGEMENT

This may sound weird, but I believe crises of faith can be wonderful things. I probably said that just to use the word *crises.* What a wonderful word. Crises. Anyway, a crisis of faith may not feel wonderful when you're in one, but afterward you can experience rewards of stronger faith and deeper peace which

> **AFTERWARD YOU CAN EXPERIENCE REWARDS OF STRONGER FAITH AND DEEPER PEACE.**

completely outweigh the temporary suffering you had to endure to get through. I'm sure everyone in Heaven thinks of earthly suffering and trials as tiny blips compared to the stretch of eternity before them now.

I wouldn't say my crisis was *the* thing that led me down the wrong path. I believe it was the fact that my church didn't really know what to do with me during that time. But honestly, how could they? How could someone lead me down a path they'd never taken? We can only take others as far as we ourselves have gone.

So if *you* are in a crisis of faith right now, I have a word for you:

Hang in there, kid. This too shall pass. There is a light at the end of this tunnel, and it is even warmer and brighter than you could ever imagine. Keep moving forward.

QUESTIONS FOR DISCUSSION AND REFLECTION

1. Have you ever felt alone or significantly different among other Christians? In what way?

2. Dave talks about "three buckets" of Christian beliefs: essential beliefs, important beliefs, and personal beliefs. Describe examples of each of the "three buckets." How have you experienced division within the church or among friends because of misplaced views within these buckets?

3. The gospel is an essential belief for all Christians. How have you or others around you moved elements of the gospel to a second or third bucket?

4. When you've had doubts in your faith, what was the critical conversation or belief that allowed you to remain a Christian?

5. Dave describes how, when he was struggling with doubt, it would have been helpful for someone to tell him, "Hang in there, kid. This too shall pass." Describe a time when someone encouraged you in your faith.

6. Dave stated that crises in faith can bring about stronger faith. When have you seen this happen in your own life or in someone close to you?

3
THE THREE UNFORGIVABLE SINS

One of my earliest memories of church was seeing one of our deacons smoking a cigarette outside the side door of the church. I turned to my mom and asked, "Is he…still a Christian?" My mom laughed nervously and said yes as she hurried me along, but I knew even at such a young age that our bodies were temples and anything we did to harm them was a sin. So, smoking? Yes, it was definitely a sin in my little brain. I would've said the same thing about tattoos at the time.

I grew up with the impression that there were three things you didn't ever do if you were a Christian: you

THERE WERE THREE THINGS YOU DIDN'T EVER DO IF YOU WERE A CHRISTIAN.

didn't drink alcohol, you didn't smoke cigarettes, and you *definitely* did not say cuss words.

These beliefs carried on into college. I mentioned earlier that I joined the Baptist Student Union my freshman year. What that meant was that I went to weekly Bible studies, worship nights, mission trips, and also tried my hardest not to sin in any way, shape, or form—specifically not in the forms of drinking, swearing, or smoking. Those three things made it LOOK like you weren't a Christian (emphasis on *look* in case you didn't catch the all-caps).

I will say that living that way kept me away from a lot of trouble, so there's that. But there is a way to abstain from those things without alienating yourself from others or setting yourself up in a position of judgment—or worse, of being in a place where you're trying to make non-Christians act Christlike.

DISCIPLESHIP BEFORE I KNEW WHAT IT WAS

As a council member at the BSU, I was required to have a weekly counseling session with one of the directors. We had two solid dudes leading the organization. The director was an old-school-style leader with a real heart for college students. He added the word SUX to that list of unspeakable words for BSU goers—which was super hard to stop saying for some reason. The associate student pastor happened to be a musician. I got to spend an hour with him every week, which was huge for me. I didn't know it at the time, but he was week-in, week-out discipling me. We would talk about music. Then there were times the conversation would go deep and I would confess some of my fears/thoughts/sins to him. They were usually met with a "me too."

He probably would've been the person to help me walk through my doubts if I had been brave enough to voice them.

But I was sort of scarred by the reaction of my peers, so I didn't really let him know about them. I guess I was worried I would be kicked off the worship team or something. I probably said the classic line of, "Yes, I have *had* doubts before…a lonnnnng time ago. But not now. I'm totally good now" to protect my current state of affairs. Through our weekly conversations, he was the first person to broaden my thinking on a lot of things outside of our Bible Belt culture.

He once mentioned to me that Christians in other countries were known to drink beer when they got together. This literally stumped me, I'm embarrassed to say. Also, when I found out my favorite author C. S. Lewis regularly met up with another favorite author of mine, J. R. R. Tolkien, at a pub to smoke pipes and drink, that was equally mind-blowing. After reading books like *Mere Christianity* and *The Problem of Pain*, it was obvious that these men knew and loved the Lord, and yet they regularly partook in something I had always considered an obvious sin.

I checked every reference for alcohol in the Bible.

It's connected with getting drunk, being caught off-guard, and…*being murdered.* Great. But then there are verses where King David thanks God for "wine that gladdens human hearts" (Psalms 104:15). Also, Paul said to "use a little wine because of your stomach and your frequent illnesses" (1 Timothy 5:23). A requirement for being an elder is "not indulging in much wine" (1 Timothy 3:8). Interesting.

I still wasn't convinced that it was okay for *me* to drink. But then my Christian pop punk band and I visited Nashville, TN, for our very first Gospel Music Awards week. There we met some very interesting people. Were we invited? Of course not, but we just kind of showed up and ate the snacks.

THE WEIRD AND WACKY WORLD THAT IS THE CHRISTIAN MUSIC INDUSTRY

I was introduced to men and women in the Christian music industry that week and it was a bit of a culture shock to this Alabama boy. Hearing them talk about the Lord and about what they were involved in with helping the needy in their city was completely invigorating. They sounded and acted a lot like the Jesus of the Bible I had in my mind during this time—gentle, humble, not easily surprised, not afraid of anything. To put it in one word, they seemed *free*.

I probably need to pause and explain to you that a big word in southern Christian culture would be the word *guilt*.

I know I often felt guilty about my own sin before God. I would be so worn down by the fact that I kept messing up with the same exact sin over and over that I couldn't fully accept the fact that I was covered in the righteousness of Christ. I won't be vague about what I'm talking about here since I'm letting everything else out in this chapter: I struggled with porn from 15 years old to age 30.

Thanks to programs like Celebrate Recovery and Sexaholics Anonymous, I can thankfully say I have been sober from that darkness for years now—*praise the Lord.* But before getting sober, I always felt like God was disappointed in me, even when I wasn't consciously sinning. Back then, I wasn't sure that I was truly saved, because how could God save someone like me? My prayers mainly consisted of "I'm sorry's" and "I'll never do that again's" on repeat.

> **I ALWAYS FELT LIKE GOD WAS DISAPPOINTED IN ME.**

These people I met in Nashville didn't seem to have that weight of guilt on them like I did. It was like they fully and completely relied on the grace of God for the full forgiveness of their sins and the salvation for their souls. Novel idea, right? I hadn't seen that before at this level. I was even more blown away when, after the events of the day, we all went to a "restaurant" called *The Flying Saucer.* I include quotation marks here because this place is known for having hundreds of beers on tap, and when you want to use code in front of legalistic Christians for "Hey, let's go drink," you say, "We're going to a restaurant later…."

The Flying Saucer allows (or allowed) you to smoke in the room as well. So, these same people who seemed to me to be so close to the character of Jesus a few hours ago were now sitting in a smoke-filled room puffing on cigars and taking big draughts of dark beer, all the while talking about theology (what a bunch of Inklings wannabes…).

I was seriously unsure if it was okay to enjoy myself. I'd love to see a replay of this night of me awkwardly walking to the bathroom trying to look like I had been in a real-life bar before, weirdly smiling and nodding at everyone on the way. What a newb. I definitely felt confused and felt a little bit of (here's that word again) *guilt.* Would God be okay with me being in this room with *these* people?

And then it happened. I absolutely could not believe it. It was one thing to hang out at a restaurant while *other* people did the sinning, but all of sudden out of nowhere, someone in our group said, "slipped and busted my a——." With those words echoing in my brain, it was at that moment that I realized I had had *enough.* I couldn't be expected to let my little virgin ears be tainted in this way, could I? If this had been a PG-13 movie, I would've promptly turned it off and proceeded to complain to anyone near me about its audacity. And yet…these people were also the closest thing I had seen to the character of Christ in my life. So, what did this mean?

I went to bed confused that night. I prayed to God about it. The next day, my bandmates and I talked about it. Some of us were excited while others were a little unsure. I had always been the mom of the band. I didn't earn the nickname "Downer Dave" for nothing, so it was no surprise that I was pretty outspoken that we *weren't* going to be like that.

GREATEST. CHRISTIAN. RAPPER. EVER.

We took a quick weekend run of shows up to Chicago and back. It wasn't every day you got the opportunity to open for THE John Reuben, so we said yes even though our van was broken down and we didn't "technically" have a way up there. We were living in an apartment in Jumpertown, MS, at this point, so that was quite the haul to Chicago. A youth pastor in Nashville that had brought us in for a show had once offered to drive us all the way up there. He was an answered prayer for sure. So, we basically spent fourteen hours in a truck with this guy.

What's funny is that, as a Christian artist, you know the fans that meet you probably have some pedestal version of you in their minds—where you don't struggle with any major sins, never doubt or question God, agree 100% with their own personal theology, and always vote Republican. I thought I wouldn't do that to anyone else from experiencing that on the other side. Yet I totally did that with our youth pastor friend.

I assumed a lot about him, so I was completely surprised when the youth pastor let his guard down and started talking and sounding *a lot* like those Christian drinker-smoker-cussers. He kept using the word *liberated.* He said that Jesus had come to liberate us from our sins and that if we were still experiencing guilt over anything, then we hadn't really accepted the fact that we'd been set free. The prison door had been open the whole time; just walk on out! To Jesus, it didn't matter when we messed up. We're humans, we do that, and God knows that. To Jesus, what was more important was that we loved God and treated the people around us well.

BITTERSWEET LIBERATION

As much as I didn't want to give in to this new way of thinking, something started loosening in me. A tightness of grip relaxed. A little blood rushed back into my years-long white-knuckle game. Was it possible to really live this way? Could God really forgive this completely? I remember a part of me beginning to want to let go of this legalistic part of my upbringing. I began to want to know what it felt like to sit in a pub enjoying a pint of dark beer, smoking a pipe, and talking about the Lord.

It was as if I had a tight grip on strings tied to multiple balloons which had kept me floating smugly above regular people on the ground. One by one, I found myself releasing those balloons from my life. Alcohol. Tobacco. Occasional cuss words (at first just to make my friends laugh). At this point in my life, I had a tight grip on my resolve to quit my addiction to pornography, but I would later relax on my personal pursuit of holiness altogether and give myself a break when I "slipped up" every other week…or day.

I began living with this leniency because I thought it didn't matter what I did anymore. Instead, what mattered was how I treated people, specifically how I treated the nonbelievers and the outcasts excluded from the American church (e.g., the sexually promiscuous, the doubters, LGBTQ's—or to sum it all up, "sinners" and "nonbelievers").

I even began to relate more to the nonbeliever than I did the average churchgoer.

I sincerely hope I haven't misled you in this chapter: I am not throwing shade on alcohol or moderate tobacco use. I'm not putting those things in the same category as obvious sins such as lust and porn. I, for one, enjoy both alcohol and pipe tobacco in moderation. I, for another one, am an aspiring Inkling (look it up). And, depending on the day, you may still hear me say a cuss word just to make a friend laugh, although generally I try my best to find better words to use than those.

The point I hope I'm clearly making is that *I slowly changed some of my own personal convictions in order to do the things I really wanted to do.*

Of course, it didn't feel like that in the moment. It never does. We have all fallen short and performed some version of doublethink on ourselves with which we switch our minds from what we ought to do to what we secretly have been wanting to do. I flipped that switch and hid it from my family and even from the churches where we put on concerts. This change further drove the wedge between me and the conservative Christian.

Honestly, it all felt a little edgy, and I was happy about it. It was sort of a rebellious feeling. Jesus even seemed more like a rebel to me during this time. In my mind, Jesus had come in order to stump the Pharisees, flip some tables, and reverse all the previously stated rules and regulations. "You have heard it said, but I tell you…"

The scary thing is that my new version of Jesus started to look only like a small portion of his real character rather than the whole thing.

Yes, Jesus is gracious, but he is also truthful. Should we even really desire him to be anything less? Think of your friendships. How fulfilling are they when someone just lets you vent to them but never pushes back on what you think and feel? Why would we want a God who is a pushover and lets us do horrible things against him and never speaks up to let us know he's offended?

JESUS IS GRACIOUS, BUT HE IS ALSO TRUTHFUL.

I think it was maybe because I had grown accustomed to the God of *only* truth that the God of *only* grace was pretty attractive. I could live how I wanted, never feel bad about it, and still believe I'd go to Heaven when I died. For the first time in my life, I actually felt…free. And the conservative Christians I had grown up around? Now, I pitied them for being so far behind when it came to true Christianity.

Isn't it interesting how the boy intent on living life differently than the "hypocritical Christians" actually grew up to be exactly like them?

That's usually what happens to self-righteous, judgmental people. It's funny (no, it's scary) how the Devil sets his traps. One minute, you're trapped in a very dark addiction and you're so low yourself that you couldn't possibly look down on anyone else. Then you seek help, get some sobriety, get baptized, memorize Scripture, and get involved in a church and small groups.

Then, long before you realize it, you're wondering why your old friends from high school aren't further along in their relationship with God (like you). And, without realizing it, you're becoming "twice the son of hell" you were before you even found God. What an awful, meticulous plan that works nearly every time. To quote a great group of theologians (Stryper): "To Hell with the Devil."

SO, WHAT DO WE DO?

Where do we find hope that we can walk Jesus' straight and narrow path? It is literally impossible on our own, but God says a thing or two about himself versus impossibilities—something about the ability to do "immeasurably more" than we can ask (Ephesians 3:20). When we're seeking and trusting him for each next step, we may still fall, but we will always get back up and walk again.

There *is* a way to live free and not be a self-righteous person with hidden sin. There *is* a way to live free and not be flippant about personal holiness. It's the way of grace *and* truth that Jesus calls us to, and he is the one who will show us how to do it. It is a road which demands more intentionality and is not without pain, but the pain is only temporary. The depth of relationship with God, the freedom in Christ's righteousness, and the warmth of friendship with the Holy Spirit by far outweigh any hardship we have to go through or any favorite sin we have to give up in order to follow Jesus.

QUESTIONS FOR DISCUSSION AND REFLECTION

1. Read Matthew 7:3-5. What is that "speck of sawdust" (a smaller sin) that really tends to drive you crazy in other people?
2. Read 1 Peter 1:15-16 and Galatians 5:19-21. Which sins of the flesh are particularly difficult to acknowledge as unholy in your own life?
3. What are the common excuses that you or others make to cover up sinful behavior?
4. What has been your experience with feelings of guilt? How has guilt been useful or not useful in your Christian walk?
5. What would it be like to have freedom from the struggles you mentioned in question 2?

Dave says, "The depth of relationship with God, the freedom in Christ's righteousness, the warmth of friendship with the Holy Spirit far outweigh any hardship we have to go through, any favorite sin we have to give up in order to follow Jesus."

6. How has this shown itself as true (or false) in your life? Give a few examples.

4
THE BANNED BOOKS AND PODCASTS

Now, I absolutely hated reading throughout high school and college. It wasn't until *The Lion, the Witch, and the Wardrobe* movie was about to come out that I decided to stop being a regular movie enjoyer and start being one of those people that reads the book (mainly to be able to complain about how bad the movie is). Yeah…one of *those* people. At any given point in time nowadays, I'm usually reading 1–3 different books, both fiction and non-fiction, and I largely credit C. S. Lewis for helping me love books.

As a kid who came to Christ early and had heard the story of Jesus since birth, it was hard to pinpoint how my heart felt when believing the gospel for the very first time. So, when I was reading *The Lion, the Witch, and the Wardrobe,* Aslan's death came out of nowhere and completely shocked me. Like a major life event, I can still remember where I was when Aslan died. And I'll also never forget the feeling I had all over my body when a few pages later he came back to life. I had tears in my eyes, and I was looking around the public library wondering if anyone else knew about this story or knew about Jesus. I was having an experience, and to the outsider looking in I probably looked like a complete weirdo. I'm fine with that.

> **I CAN STILL REMEMBER WHERE I WAS WHEN ASLAN DIED.**

That moment in Narnia was kind of like hearing the gospel again for the first time for me. For that experience, I'm forever grateful for Lewis's allegorical story. And to the Columbus Public Library: I'm sorry for being the weird young man crying upstairs reading children's books.

After *Narnia,* I picked up *Mere Christianity,* where I learned about how my innermost moral code was proof outside the Bible for the existence of God. I discovered that if time was a line on a page, then, far from being on the line, God would be the page itself (insert your favorite mind-blown GIF here). Then I raced through *The Great Divorce,* where I learned that our eternal destinies are the result of the little decisions we make every day. When we arrive in eternity, it'll feel like we've always been there because we have been choosing and inviting either heaven or hell into our world little by little, every single day.

Those books changed the way I thought about God and sparked a desire to know more about him through literature.

NOW WE'RE GOING TO TALK ABOUT ROB BELL

It wasn't too long after my journey through Lewis's material that I watched my first *NOOMA* video during a church small group meeting. These were ten-minute devotional videos featuring mini-sermons from the one and only Rob Bell.

Disclaimer: I probably know what you're thinking: *I knew it! That darned, west coast Rob Bell guy is at it again! He's the reason that Stovall boy lost his faith! I knew that Bell was trouble!* I want to say this before continuing: I never wanted to be a Bell hater and I still don't. I was hesitant to mention his name because I don't think it's fair to blame him for my progressivism, although he certainly has been a well-known progressive for a number of years now. His writings did have an effect on me for sure, but some of his thoughts were genuinely helpful. I still respect him as an innovator and communicator. (By the way, Rob, if you're reading this, hit me up and I'll take you to Mojos Tacos, my treat.)

So, when I became familiar with Bell's *NOOMA* devotional videos, I could not get enough of them. They were revolutionary for me on many levels. The things Bell was saying sort of took me to a new place spiritually. It helped me see the beauty of the storytelling in the library that is the Bible. It made me think of my own mortality and whether I was using my life for anything good or just for myself. It raised the bar for me when it comes to what you could do with art and literature to tell people a story about God.

I picked up his book *Velvet Elvis.* I remember so many people telling me not to read Bell's books because they were "heretical," yet these same people had never actually read any of his books, only the reviews. So somehow their warnings actually drove me toward this stuff. It's like I was thinking, *Well, they don't like these books and I'm not like them anymore, so these books must be awesome. There must be truths here that are frightening to people who never want to be challenged or pushed.*

Right off the bat with Velvet Elvis, Bell describes having a "trampoline faith" (meaning, if you remove one metaphorical spring of theology from the trampoline, it doesn't collapse and you can keep jumping) versus having a "brick wall faith" (where if one low brick is removed, the whole wall comes tumbling down). That idea was revolutionary for me at that time. I had already been sensing that the theology of my upbringing wasn't proving to be as solid as I had been told, and I was starting to wonder if the whole thing would eventually just crumble for me. Learning that I could carry some of the harder-to-digest Bible stuff in an open hand while moving forward gave me some hope.

Using one of Bell's examples of "trampoline theology," let's say that we find out one day that Jesus had a real dad named Larry. Let's say that the virgin birth of Mary was really just a little mythology sprinkled in by the New Testament writers to appeal to followers of a certain religious cult during that time period that ascribed their gods to virgin births. Bell went further to speculate, what if we found out that the word *virgin* in the original Greek could also mean "the first sexual encounter with the husband."

"COULD ALSO MEAN…"

Those three words along with the *what ifs* in that scenario ended up creating a deeper sense of doubt in the whole thing for me. Before that moment, I had not questioned who had written the Bible. If you had asked me who wrote it, I would've answered, "God, of course," which had worked in Sunday School. Out in the real world, that answer wasn't working anymore. In fact, those three words ("could also mean") became the theological theme I was most interested in knowing about.

I learned that Paul *could have meant* pedophilic relationships when he talked about men exchanging natural for unnatural sexual relations in his letter to the church in Rome. It also became *possible* that the culture back then had a problem with homosexuality only because they had seen abusive homosexual relationships and had never seen a loving relationship between same sexes. Those sections of the Bible could have gotten it wrong because their culture wasn't as enlightened as ours is now.

I learned from progressive thinkers that things like the creation story don't have to be literally true for there to be truth in them. For example, these thinkers explained that it didn't matter if Genesis literally happened because we reenact the story of the Fall every day when we sin; therefore, the Fall is true at a level deeper than literal. Of course, that's a subtle shifting of what truth means. I also learned that Paul was the only apostle who had never seen the physical Jesus, and I began to wonder if the letters he wrote should have real authority like the writings by other (real) apostles.…

Ironically, I sort of felt like Rob had poked out a bottom brick in my own faith brick wall. The whole thing didn't come down immediately, but it sure felt shaky. However, at this point, this shakiness actually felt like a welcome relief. I could finally stop trying to explain how God was somehow love yet didn't have enough of it to go around for gay people.

> **THIS SHAKINESS ACTUALLY FELT LIKE A WELCOME RELIEF.**

THE ALLURE OF PROGRESSIVISM

For just a second, I'm going to skip ahead in my story to right after my first "reconstruction" (when my faith was officially reconstructed into the mold of progressivism).

Since this chapter is about books and podcasts (and podcasts weren't as much of a thing when I was deconstructing), I want to mention one podcast. It was literally saying the words that were floating around in my head during my deconstruction—except that the hosts were saying them in extremely entertaining ways. (This podcast was created by Christian artists, by the way, and I'll explain the attraction I've often seen between Christian artists and progressivism in the next chapter.) Somewhere along my journey of deconstructing, I started listening to *The Liturgists*. First off, *The Liturgists* podcast is extremely well done. I mean, the music alone is incredible (thanks to the brilliant, artistic mind of Michael Gungor), and their stories and content completely pull you in. The fact is, it's done so well that you may not even realize that the hosts are discussing unorthodox theologies because they are talked about in ways familiar enough to your brain to make you think they're right and true.

One of the first episodes of *The Liturgists* was about Science Mike's deconversion story. It is a very captivating story. Mike went through a deconversion in his mind before telling anyone. After a season of going through the motions of being a body in a church he no longer agreed with, he finally told his wife that he was an atheist. She was devastated. Sometime later he went on a trip and had an incredible mystical experience with God on a beach. This supernatural experience (which I think really happened) jolted him awake spiritually. Yet, as a person who relies more on their own intellect than the authoritative Word of God, he made a crucial mistake in my opinion. It was a mistake that I would go on to make myself.

Mike rationalized this newfound belief in the supernatural God by breaking down Christianity to its basic beliefs and then deciding which of those beliefs he could accept moving forward. He called them "axioms." As someone who was walking away from a faith I grew up in, I found this compromising approach to be music to my ears. I told you early on that I never desired to walk away from my faith. I wanted to stay, but I needed it to satisfy my intellect a little more than it was doing. I was afraid that there wouldn't be a way to grow in intelligence without becoming agnostic or an atheist. So, to hear that there was a way forward, a new way that included both faith in God and rational thought, was a huge relief to me.

But now, in retrospect, I realize what Science Mike did, what I did, and what most progressives do in order to stay in the faith of their childhood was reduce it down to the more tolerable teachings of the Bible and just go with those. We sort of skipped over the rest of the Bible without actually calling it *ignoring*. Rather, we would describe *those* parts as "written for that time period/culture and not ours" or as a metaphorical teaching rather than literal. And I, along with other progressives, really believed that was the case. I want to be clear that I do believe there are parts of the Bible meant to apply only in the author's culture and time period (as a Gentile, I can eat as much bacon as I want), and that there are parts of it that are not to be taken literally but metaphorically or typologically. Yet as a progressive I was doing that with *much* of the Bible—much of the meat of the Bible. And now suddenly I'm hungry…

THE GREAT AUTHORITY SWAP

To say it plainly, it was a switching of roles. Even if it didn't feel like it at the time, this cherry-picking was switching the authority of God's Word for the authority of my own intellect.

I am amazed now that I placed my own thoughts, feelings, and beliefs over the Bible—when literally all throughout history there have been Christians who have done the opposite and sacrificed as a result. People have died because they followed God's word as *the* truth. If there had been an option to stay a Christian without following all the teachings of Jesus and his words through the apostles (yes, including the apostle Paul), don't you think they would've opted for that over persecution and death?

What happens today is truth is made relative and everyone ends up happy with their own customized version of an ancient faith that looks very little like the original. There I was, a 21st-century Westerner reading the Bible through the lens of my own feelings to decipher what was true and what was "for that time period." How was my faith going to match "the faith that was once for all entrusted to God's holy people" (Jude 1:3)?

For instance, I had always known and believed homosexuality was a sin, but then I befriended gay people and heard their heartbreaking stories of being abandoned by family and being bullied—and I began to feel like there was no way a loving God would reject them too. I had always thought drinking was a sin, but then I hung around some genuine believers who drank and got tipsy, and I felt like Jesus wouldn't make them stop living that way because they had good hearts. I had always believed Old Testament stories like Jonah getting swallowed by a big fish happened literally, but when I read those stories through my scientific-American lens, they felt more like fairy tales with a moral to me. What I felt determined what I believed. The truth of the Bible just wasn't lining up with the truth of my culture anymore, or the truth of my gut.

> **WHAT I FELT DETERMINED WHAT I BELIEVED.**

PUSH YOUR NERDY GLASSES BACK UP YOUR FACE

I want to throw out a big nerdy word for you: *hermeneutic.* I had always sort of laughed at people who used that word, but here I go. I'm about to be one of those nerds. "Hermeneutics" is the study of interpretation (e.g., how to interpret the Bible). A person's "hermeneutic" basically means that person's theological framework for reading the Bible. Every human being who picks up the Bible to read it has a framework in their mind. It is a set of rules within our minds that we bring with us to Scripture to find out what it means. It's usually shaped by experiences and thoughts that we've picked up along the way. Since having a hermeneutic is inescapable, it may sound relatively insignificant, but knowing the hermeneutic you are using is extremely important. Your hermeneutic can determine how you read the Bible and what you do with it.

Here are a couple examples. Some people read the Bible with a hermeneutic that says, "If the New Testament doesn't explicitly *permit* it, then we can't do it." Therefore, they might read the New Testament and come away demanding that their church not use musical instruments since musical instruments aren't commanded for worship in the New Testament. Instead, they'll use only their voices in worship. Others might come to the Bible with a hermeneutic that says, "If the New Testament doesn't explicitly *prohibit* it, then it's up to our preferences." Therefore, they might end up saying there's gray area when it comes to using instruments in church, so let's use the creativity and resources the Lord has given us and include beautiful musical instruments in our church. Does that make sense how a person's hermeneutic determines how they read the text?

Some of my hermeneutic had always subconsciously gone something like this:

1. God wrote the Bible, so
2. The Bible should be taken literally, and
3. It can never be wrong.

That framework led me to adopt a premillennial dispensationalist view. It also led me to believe in a literal six-day creation. In fact, if I'm being honest, it led me to an unwillingness to even look at or wrestle with scientific facts that seemed to contradict the Bible. When I read these progressive books during the 2000s, it subtly shifted my hermeneutic away from my more literalistic way of reading the Bible. It was a subconscious shift. At the time, it felt like an uneasy wrestling in my mind over each issue, and I definitely felt like I was becoming more *enlightened* by this material. What was really happening was a fundamental shift in my hermeneutic which actually made the outcome of my reading of the Bible predictable. I traded a hermeneutic built on an easy literalism for a hermeneutic built on self-inspired theology. If you really want to know what the Bible says and means, it takes work and humility, but thankfully there are plenty of tools to help.

The subtleness of this shift is why we say at Renew.org that everyone is being discipled by something whether they realize it or not. As I was reading progressive authors, affirming thoughts were constantly popping up in my mind, such as, *I've never thought of it like that before. I've never heard anyone saying it like this before. This makes more sense this way.* I know now, after reconverting to historic Christianity, that those statements are actually red flags.

The Christian faith is 2,000 years old. Sure, there are going to be new discoveries when it comes to historical background, the Greek language, etc. as we move forward. But if we're coming to the text with a predetermined agenda and obsessing over sub-meanings of Greek words that *could* mean something different than what the intended original audience thought, then we should pause and think about the weight of what we're doing and the hidden purposes we may have in our own hearts. Yes, God knows our hearts (Psalm 44:21), and guess what the Creator of human hearts says about them? They're evil (Jeremiah 17:9).

Today, I still love to listen to podcasts, but I'm selective of what goes into my brain.

CONSCIOUS SATURATION

As I have moved back to historic Christianity, someone at my church asked me if I felt I had been brainwashed into coming back. I paused and thought about it before answering. While I had been listening to and reading progressive Christian material, I wouldn't have told you I was looking for another way to do Christianity, but in reality that's what I was doing. I had felt stuck and needed to find a new way forward. The things I was hearing through these various voices sounded right and true and good to me. It felt good to lose the extra baggage which my Bible Belt upbringing had placed on me. In other words, I secretly wanted a change and therefore sought out content that supported this new longing and belief within myself.

So, I answered my friend, "Here's the thing. Before, I subconsciously brainwashed myself into walking away from orthodoxy. Now, I have seen the truth again but with new eyes. I am convinced again of the truth of the gospel and of all 66 books in the Holy Bible. So, yes, I am currently saturating myself in the truth so that nothing else contrary to that works itself into my mind again." I want a fortress around my thoughts, a "helmet of salvation," if you will. I know the truth, and I also know how easy it is to be persuaded away from it by my own feelings. So, I am doing what God tells me to do by taking every thought captive and making it obedient to Christ (2 Corinthians 10:5).

Is making every thought obedient to Christ something I ultimately want for myself? Absolutely. Does it feel good and right every time there is a new instance where the commands of the Bible don't line up with what I want or what my culture tells me is right? Absolutely not. But I have learned that the only way forward through doubts and questions is obedient trust. I lean into what God tells me in his Word even though it can sound upside down. And every single time, it turns out to be the best thing for me and also for those around me. You can only experience that if you lean into the Bible's truthfulness and therefore walk in its light. It's not easy, but, man, it is good and worth it.

My encouragement to you is this: don't let yourself be someone who is unknowingly being discipled by the world by letting it shape your thoughts and feelings so that they determine what you can and can't seem to believe in. Please read that last sentence again because it's my most important one in this chapter.

Also, please don't misunderstand the progressive Christian as someone who is only trying their hardest to fit in with the culture as if it were a popularity contest. I would say that at least some of them are genuinely trying to find the truth and believe they have found it in a new way of thinking and interpreting the Bible. Some are quite humble about their position. If you are someone who wants to reach a progressive Christian and bring them back to submitting to the lordship of Jesus we find in all of Scripture, the place to start is not by criticizing their tactics for justifying what they want to do by twisting Scripture. That stuff is usually happening under the surface, and they may not even be aware of it. We need to love progressives enough to go into the hard conversations with them. Let's be curious about how they think. Let's be innocent as doves as well as shrewd as snakes (Matthew 10:16).

I for one study the truth in Scripture and memorize facts about the Bible, but I also keep an ear to the ground for what's going on in progressive Christianity. I don't want to be clueless as to what's happening because my goal is to lovingly lead people back. In my experience, in the Christian music industry, there were loads of people being pulled in this direction. In fact, I might even say the lifestyle you have to live in order to work that career sort of lends itself to making artists into walking dichotomies. You have your real inner self with the questions and the outward brand version of you that everyone expects and buys. It can split you in two and leave you a jaded person toward the faith.

I was one of those broken people. And you know who has a big heart for broken people? Our Lord and Savior, Jesus Christ. I want to have his heart, and I want to be his hands to lift those brothers and sisters back up and bring them home. I hope as you continue to read this book that you will be that person too. The further our culture drifts into post-Christian beliefs and assumptions, we're going to need all the help we can get.

QUESTIONS FOR DISCUSSION AND REFLECTION

1. What are some of your favorite Christian influences in your life (podcast, YouTube channel, author)? How deep of a dive have you made to determine if they are upholding the authority of Scripture or undermining it?
2. If you want to keep (or return to) a healthy respect for the authority of Scripture, what are some helpful parameters you should set for the content you allow into your mind?
3. What does it mean to trust the authority of Scripture over our feelings?
4. Have you ever used the phrase "God knows the heart" to justify sin in your own life or someone else's? In what context?
5. Read Jeremiah 17:9. What does God tell us about ourselves in this passage?
6. What change can you make this week to begin saturating yourself in the things of God more than in the things of the world?

5
FROM EMOTIONALISM TO CYNICISM

The youth minister finishes up his fifteen-minute sermon and then pauses for dramatic effect after closing his Bible. He swallows and slowly raises his eyes from the floor to look at his youth group and takes a deep breath. "Kids, I just wanna tell you—and I ain't tryna scare you, I'm just saying it like it is....You could die tomorrow. Shoot, you could die on the way home from church to-NIGHT!" He pauses and then relieves the heavy silence by saying, "Where're you gonna spend eternity—in heaven with Jesus...or forever in hell with the worms that never die?" And with an almost imperceptible head nod, he cues what my bandmates and I have since nicknamed "The Holy Ghost Fog Machine," and we know that's also our cue to play a song which will be dramatic enough to make the kids feel just guilty enough to make a decision for Christ.

I want you to know I have written, scrapped, and rewritten this chapter four times now. I don't know how to say it. I'm not sure I *want* to say it, but I am convinced it needs to be written. I started writing my story under a compulsion that God wants me to share it, not to try to elevate myself somehow or bring anyone else down.

Yet just as I've been unflatteringly honest about myself throughout this series, part of my story involves some sober reflections about the music industry that has played such a prominent role in my life. The Contemporary Christian Music industry, or what I will refer to as CCM for the rest of this chapter, played a major part in my story, and so I have to include it here. But I'm not trying to make this any kind of sensational exposé of the industry. Just my reflections—some good, some bad—and from my perspective only. Sound fair? Okay, let's proceed.

DISCOVERING CHRISTIAN ROCK

From as early as the age of five, I can remember wanting to be an entertainer. Back then, I was listening to MJ's *Thriller* and *Off the Wall* albums. So, when my Sunday school teachers would ask me what I wanted to be when I grew up, I would say, "I'm going to be a singer and dancer." Then they would reply something like, "That's nice, little David. Maybe that's what God will have for you. We'll see!" That statement turned into, "That's nice, but... have a backup plan" as I grew older.

When I was fifteen, my world was rocked. I had been listening to Stryper ("To Hell with the Devil") and a little hip-hop Christian group called dc Talk. I can actually remember exactly where I was when their album *Jesus Freak* came out. We were driving away from the Barnes Crossing Mall in Tupelo, MS, and I popped this new thing called a Compact Disc into my black/blue Sony Discman, and my ears came alive to the sound of Toby Mac whispering "I got something for ya, maaaan." I paused after the "Jesus Freak" track and looked at my mom and said, "Mom...I'm not sure if I'm supposed to be listening to this. It sounds... secular." We listened to *Christian music only* in our family—well, plus a little Michael Jackson...and Chicago...and Hall and Oates. So, this Christian grunge music was new, and it sort of (Jesus) freaked me out.

My parents did the right thing that all totally awesome musician parents do: they bought tickets to the next dc Talk show in Nashville, TN. The opening act was a little rock 'n' roll band called Audio Adrenaline (wink).

Up until that point, I already knew I wanted to be an entertainer, but after Will McGuiness head-banged that bleach-blond hair of his while ripping up sick bass lines for an hour and Toby Mac dove off the high speakers into the crowd, I had

I WANTED TO ROCK... FOR THE ROCK.

a new direction for my calling: I wanted to rock...for *the* Rock. I no longer wanted to have my mom hem my slacks high enough to show off my sequin socks that matched my one glove; I wanted to jam for the Lamb and rock skulls for the One who died at Skull Rock (okay, okay; I'll stop). I wanted my gift to be used by God to spread the Good News across the whole planet.

GETTING SIGNED

In my late teen years, I started recording music on a digital recording machine with a 1" by 6" screen (before MacBooks came out and made it easy to sound good). Then in college I started my first band. Although we met some great people, my bandmates and I realized pretty quickly that not everyone in the Christian music industry handled their business in a Christ-like manner. (In fact, there have been some occasions where the CCM world has actually been more cut-throat than the mainstream/secular music world!)

Right off the bat, we got some shows with a pretty big Christian band, and we were so pumped. Then we saw how big of douchebags these band members were to the sound teams at several churches where we played with them. We cringed as the singer, during a show right in front of their fans, threw his hands up in frustration at the tech team when the breakers blew and the power turned off. We decided we wouldn't be that way and that this particular band had come into our lives to show us how *not* to be a Christian band.

Another example of early disillusionment: when we came into the studio, we did some co-writing sessions where other musical artists came in, edited or arranged our songs, and then demanded a super high percentage cut of the writer's share. We were the little guys, but we didn't want to get stepped on, so we stood up to them and ended up getting what was fair. But we also felt like we got blacklisted by their management company for the remainder of our career. It became clear that the options were to either be taken advantage of or be rejected for possible touring options in the future. We did end up getting signed to a record label, but far from being a satisfying experience, getting signed—and then dropped just as quickly—revealed more of a corporate machine than a Christ-centered ministry.

Some Christian artists have a fruitful, healthy relationship with the CCM industry, but it is sad to see many promising Christian artists enter the industry only to witness disappointingly un-Christian elements. Some of our own fans have wondered what happened to us and why we stopped calling ourselves a "Christian" band....Well, when you get disillusioned over and over by an industry which you thought was going to be more about Jesus than it ended up being, it sort of messes you up. You start thinking you don't want anything to do with an industry that can feel so corrupt and be all about sales. I honestly think that's why we see so many former Christian band members become alcoholics, sex addicts, drug users, and even cynics who lose their light and end up walking away from the faith altogether. It's hard stuff to process. Sometimes it damages you for good.

THE TRUTH ABOUT CHRISTIAN ARTISTS

Here's the truth about Christian artists: they are broken people just like you except that they keep getting placed on these high pedestals in the minds of their fans. Just like us, these singers and musicians don't have it all figured out. They don't have all the answers. They just want to bless God and people through their art. They are also trying to make a living with their skills like everyone else and so they have to make certain decisions based on that fact. What's more is that they have less time to be connected to a local church and therefore are much more likely to isolate their doubts and questions and end up in heretical places of thinking and theology.

They need real relationships with real people who are not super fans. In fact, super fans are exactly what they *don't* need; what they need are followers of Jesus in their closest circle that can speak truth to them. They need real, life-on-life small group discipleship on a regular basis with someone more mature in the Christian faith than they are.

When we ignore the fact that all Christians are broken people (pastors, artists, etc.) and treat them like super-Christians, we further feed their impulse to stay silent about who they are and how they really think and feel. Maybe instead of getting your poster signed this one time, shake their hand and ask them how you can be praying for them. Encourage them to stay in the Word and remain in Jesus. Side note: probably the quickest way to gain audience with a Christian superstar is to ask them to go out for drinks after the show. That's almost like code language for "Hey, I'm not a super-fan, I just want to know who you really are and see if you're doing okay."

I was never a famous Christian artist. I guess I could say I was "small town famous," but that didn't stop people from putting even me on a pedestal. A couple small examples: a bandmate and I once made the mistake of mentioning we had seen *Gone Girl* in front of someone who was interviewing us, and their eyebrows raised as they judgmentally asked, "You…you like *those kind* of movies?"

I also had a minister bring me up on stage after leading worship for them only to thank me and say, "People always said Dave was crazy"—pause for medium crowd giggling—"…crazy about Jesus." This moment actually almost made me break right there in front of everyone because, little did they know, I had been doubting earlier that day if I even really knew Jesus.

No one would ask me how I was really doing. Most people want (or maybe even need) us to be "on" when we have an interaction with them; almost

> **NO ONE WOULD ASK ME HOW I WAS REALLY DOING.**

like they need us, as people on the "inside," to confirm that the faith is real and worth it. You know those people that ask you a question but their phrasing and facial expressions are all about trying to get the answer they want to hear out of you? Yeah. That kind of checking up on me would happen all the time—but never the real stuff.

LEAVING THE CHRISTIAN MUSIC WORLD

So, there's this splitting of the soul that can happen for the Christian artist. On the one hand, you need to be authentic and real because you're creating and selling art with God's name on it. On the other hand, you need to be what your consumers are paying good money for you to be and what they (sometimes desperately) need you to be. I feel icky just talking about it.

Our band Wavorly got to a place where we wanted to be authentic with our music, our lives, and our industry. Yet at the time, there wasn't really a place for that in the Christian music world for us. We ended up leaving it behind to pursue the mainstream market (a.k.a., the secular market). We stopped playing as many shows in churches and started playing in bars. I actually felt more at home with the "real people" I found in the bar scene. They were sharing real stories, the nitty gritty. Some of them had lost everything, and they were there just to drink a beer and have a good conversation. Fertile ground for the gospel, I'd say. It makes sense why Jesus spent time with broken people like that.

So, we went from getting well taken care of by the old ladies at churches across the country to playing at dark and sweaty bars with owners who couldn't care less about another no-name band coming through. So, we made these places our mission field. I felt like we were doing "the real" Lord's work—not just serving Christians but reaching the lost.

And that's an honorable goal. Plenty of bands went down this road before us, and on that road, plenty of bands burned out and broke up as we would eventually do. Playing in bars was freeing at first. I said things like, "I'd much rather play for 50 people in a bar than 300 people in a church. It's way more real here." What I felt and what I meant was a level of authenticity expressed by the people in a bar as well as a level of authenticity within myself that I could now reveal at places like this.

I could say I was struggling with doubt and had some serious questions about the faith. If I wanted to say a low-key swear word at the merch table, I could—we were in a bar! The people there were much less interested in trapping you in your theology or in looking down on your list of preferred Christian authors. They cared about one thing: your *story*. Remember that word for a minute. This is where we're going to get into the weeds a little bit.

I felt like I was doing the Lord's work by singing in bars to drunk (or on the way to being drunk) people and talking with them afterwards over a drink or four. Jesus hung out with sinners, right? I just wanted to do the same. But if I'm being honest, there was one major thing missing when I was "ministering" to these lost people: the gospel.

IMMERSED IN PROGRESSIVE CHRISTIANITY

When Jesus spent time with sinners, he was hearing their story, treating them as real human beings, and then casting a vision for a *better* way (*the* way, actually). He accepted them where they were but invited them on this journey of following him and changing to become more and more like him. The best thing for anyone that's ever existed is to surrender their life to their Creator and let him call the shots. He knows what's up.

But it was at this time that I was immersed in progressive Christianity. I had gotten here by reacting against the legalism of my past, getting burnt by the disillusionment of much of evangelical Christianity, and finding a freer, more authentic version of Christianity in progressive authors. And, in my experience, inviting people into a gospel which calls us to sacrificially follow Jesus is an area that is seriously lacking in progressive Christianity. Progressives usually say, "Come as you are; however you are is just fine," instead of, "Come as you are, and we'll help you become more like Jesus."

So, I would talk with these people at the bar, hear their stories, share my story, and watch them be amazed that a Christian was hanging out in a bar with a non-Christian while not trying to judge or convert them. Looking back, I think that sort of became my mission: to show the world that I'm not really different from them....

That kind of mission *sounds* sort of right—until you realize that it's actually the opposite of what we see in the Bible. How many examples and stories are there in the Old Testament describing how God set apart a special people unto himself? How much of that did I have to forget to get to a place of trying to be a Christian who is basically indistinguishable from the world? We were meant to be *holy* as God is holy (1 Peter 1:16). God is still interested in transforming lives so that his people stop sinning and wholly take on his character as their own.

If you're keeping up with the story, what you're seeing now is how I made a long trip from a Christianity of truth and nothing but the judgmental truth, all the way over to grace, grace, and absolutely nothing else but grace. I came to feel that these nonbelievers were basically good people. After all, they were created in the image of God, and therefore he loved them. And that is true, but only a part of the whole truth.

God loves them so, so much (more than they could even know) that he laid his life down for them. But why did he lay his life down for them? It was not so they could stay dead in their sin patterns which bring nothing but death and destruction to themselves and the ones they

THE WHOLE GOSPEL IS BEAUTIFUL AND PURE.

love. Jesus died so that they could experience real, satisfying, and transformed living—here on earth and in heaven after leaving this world. The whole gospel is beautiful and pure. The half gospel you get in progressivism sounds and feels nice but ends up being empty.

A RECOVERING SKEPTIC

In his eye-opening book *A Grand Illusion,* my friend David Young describes how some people use progressivism as an on-ramp to get people into Christianity when in actuality it is an off-ramp *from* Christianity. I know that sounds harsh, but I believe it to be true and definitely have experienced it.

While I was deconstructing, I came across a bullet-point list online written by a man who grew up in the evangelical world but is now an atheist. He basically described my childhood, my experience in youth group, and the same doubts and questions I had in college. As I looked at each step he took away from the faith of his childhood all the way down to the bottom of the list, I was shocked when I realized that I myself was only a few steps away from agnosticism and eventually (where the author landed) atheism. This truly scared me. I said earlier that during my trip through progressivism I felt more enlightened—like I was waking up. Seeing the end of the road shook something loose in my thinking about progressive Christianity. I'm hoping as you're reading this book it will do the same for you.

Lately I have been introducing myself to people as a recovering skeptic. I get it; there are many, many questions about God and Christianity that we will probably never have figured out this side of heaven. I don't try to pretend that mysteries surrounding God don't exist. In fact, I try my best to embrace it. I believe Jesus is big enough to handle any and all of our questions and doubts.

A friend of mine describes this as a landing place called the "second naïveté." I acknowledge that, on one hand, there are still a lot of really tough questions about God, the Bible, and Jesus that puzzle me, and on the other I still completely trust that God is good enough, big enough, and smart enough to handle those mysteries. God deserves the benefit of the doubt when we're wrestling with questions about his character and/or his actions. He already knows our thoughts, so why not bring them out in the open before him and let him help us work it out?

A THIRD WAY

Here's my encouragement, my challenge, my plea to you (whether you are a fundamentalist, a progressive, a non-believer, or a long-time disciple): what would it look like for you to fully believe and trust in the *whole* gospel again?

By the whole gospel, I mean: God created the world. The world sinned. God separated his holy self from our sinful selves until a time that would come where he would lay down his own life to be brutally murdered and sacrificed to pay the massive debt that we owed. Jesus came back to life again in order to begin restoring and reconciling mankind and the whole order of creation back to God. Right now, Jesus reigns as king over those of us who follow him, and he will eventually return and restore all things to their original, glorious design.

What would change in your life and in your heart if you opened up your mind for the first time or once again to the possibility that the stories in the Bible are true? That the *whole* gospel is the good news we've been longing for? That there really is hope for victory over the darkness, and that it's found in King Jesus?

What if there was a third way that wasn't ignorantly blissful about Christianity's history and dismissive about thought-provoking questions about God and the Bible—but also not cynically walled off from the only one in whom we find solid reasons for hope? What if this middle roadway was actually the way Jesus designed for us to walk with him?

I believe God created our intellects for mentally wrestling with deep truths *with* him. Why else would God name his people "Fighter of God" ("Israel" means those who wrestle with God)? There is a way to surrender to the truth of Scripture, to submit to Jesus' lordship, and also still use your brain and intellectually satisfy most of your questions about the hot topics of the faith.

I believe that the men who discipled me have found this way. They're not perfect, but they're trying their best to be honest with themselves and those around them as they walk humbly with faith. It's beautiful, actually. This honest yet hopeful faith is a lot sturdier and more satisfying than either the fog-machine emotionalism or the jaded cynicism that led me down paths of disappointment.

QUESTIONS FOR DISCUSSION AND REFLECTION

1. Do you have an opinion about the contemporary Christian music industry? Pros? Cons?

2. What Christian recording artist do you consider your favorite? How might it change the way you listened to their music or enjoyed their shows if you were to accept the fact that even famous artists are just regular, everyday people fighting through the Christian life like you?

3. Who in your life is the person you can be completely authentic with, especially with regard to your Christian walk?

4. Does this relationship (in question 3) allow you to stay in the sin struggle or encourage you toward holiness?

5. Think of some of the non-believers in your life; hold them in your mind. Take some time to pray that God would intervene in your lost friends' lives and save them. Ask God to use you in their lives and to help you pay attention to when he wants you to open your mouth and speak the truth to them.

6. What is holding you back from allowing the Holy Spirit to lead in your life? Describe those obstacles and confess them to the Lord.

6
THE FLEETING FULFILLMENT OF A FEELINGS-BASED FAITH

Something changed in me the day my first child was born back in 2016. In a lot of ways, being a dad for the first time brought on a lot of pressure. But there was a different form of pressure that fell off me when I first laid eyes on my son: I felt like I finally understood grace and saw how big it was.

I looked at this helpless little person in my hands and was compelled to love that baby boy with all that I am no matter what. If he grew up to hate me, I would still love him. If he grew up to be an atheist, I would still love him. If he grew up to be a womanizer or a drug user or a porn addict, I would still love him. That is exactly the way God feels about you and about me. The father of the prodigal son never stopped loving his son. Can I say that again so that it sinks in? God made you and he delights in you. Believe that. Live free in that truth.

SO, WHAT DO I TEACH MY KID?

As time moved on and my boy, Bear, got older, I began to really enjoy teaching him new things as all dads do. One day, as I was holding him in his room rocking him to sleep, I wondered what I would teach him about God. This was when I was still a progressive, so I knew I didn't want to teach him the tradition of Christianity that I grew up with. But would I show him the fuzzy freedom and grace-with-no-strings-attached that I had found in progressivism? How do you even teach that?

In progressivism, there were too many unanswered riddles for a child to understand—too much gray area. I'm told children need black or white. My wife and I found this out the hard way by allowing our son to say the word "fart" only inside our home when he was around three years old. It went something like this:

"Bear, can you hand me your cup?"

"Well, farty fartskins, I sure farty can, ya fart!"

Gray area just doesn't compute in children's tiny developing minds. In my experience, progressive Christianity is all about the gray. All it would take to watch progressive theology fall apart in the mind of a child would be for my son to ask, "Why did Jesus have to die?" The only answer progressive Christianity gave me was, "We're not really sure…"

The Bible teaches (as does Jesus himself) that the reason he came to this world was to die, be lifted up, defeat Satan, and draw every man, woman, and child to himself (John 12:31–32). Then this theme is fleshed out even more through the apostle Paul's writings to the Romans, that "we are made right with God by placing our faith in Jesus Christ" (Romans 3:22a, NLT).

It's a message simple enough for even a child to understand, but progressive Christianity had me second-guessing the purpose of Jesus' death by getting me to doubt the authority of Paul. When I accepted that he was not a *real* apostle because he wasn't with Jesus before he died, Paul became just another learner like myself, and his writings didn't really hold the same weight that Jesus' words did anymore. This is what it looks like to be a "red letter Christian," who ends up saying things like, "I'm good with Jesus but not much else."

MY PROBLEM WITH PAUL

The first time I heard Paul's authority questioned like that was pretty earthshattering. "Wow. So much of his writing makes sense now that I know he was just trying to figure it out like I am." I went from literally believing everything in the Bible to questioning about half of the New Testament. I would read passages like 1 Corinthians 14:34 ("Women should remain silent in the churches.

They are not allowed to speak, but must be in submission, as the law says"), and I would take it out, examine it, and decide if it made sense with the world around me. If it didn't, I would tuck it right back where I found it, never to give it a second thought.

Distrusting Paul was the beginning of my distrust of the Bible as God's infallible Word as a whole. It can seem like a subtle shift to start thinking that Paul's words shouldn't carry as much weight as Jesus' or Peter's, but that shift took me all the way to where I was writing off huge chunks of the Old Testament as well.

> **IT CAN SEEM LIKE A SUBTLE SHIFT.**

Take Jonah for example. That book has the weirdest ending in the whole Bible. A plant instantly grew out of the ground to give Jonah shade, but then, when Jonah got happy about it, God caused it to die just as quickly as it had grown, and then Jonah got ticked! On the surface, it sounded to me like a comical ending to a fictional story with a moral. Since that's what it sounded like to me, I believed it had to be fiction and then moved on. It was as simple as that. I didn't realize until later that I was arrogantly canceling a lot of rich stories rooted in the long history of a very real nation of Israel.

It was almost like I had traded the lens which I looked through to read Scripture. I had switched from the everything-is-literal lens to the polar opposite, toss-it-if-it-doesn't-make-sense lens. I was making fun of the Christians who cherry-picked verses to support their ideologies even though I was doing the same thing but on different cherry trees. Even though the Bible is a collection of Ancient Near Eastern books, anything that didn't exactly line up with my 21st century Western Christian mind basically got ignored.

It's amazing that here in this beautiful country we have all sorts of free time to sit around and ponder things like theology. And right there is where we find a pretty scary part of the history of progressivism that still gives me the creeps to this day.

Again in *A Grand Illusion,* David points out the Western, elite, and almost exclusively *white* beginnings of progressivism. He talks about how only the wealthy have time to sit around and twist their thoughts about what's true and untrue about the Bible. Contrast that with people in third-world countries (or even people in cities with high poverty here in the States) who are hanging on for dear life to every word of the gospel as *the* way, *the* truth and *the* life.

If you're a progressive, I hope that makes you stop and think. Do yourself a favor and read *A Grand Illusion.* When I was a progressive, I was proud of the fact that I had an open mind. I challenge you to let yourself be open-minded to the truths you find in that book about what you believe and let it freak you out a little bit.

Give your new theology the same line of scrutiny you once gave the Bible when you were deconstructing.

I also hope this book can be a way for me to tell you more than just my story of leaving progressivism. I'd like for it also to be a way for me to help historic Christians understand the way progressives think (how they got there, the kind of beliefs their hermeneutics lead to). And also I hope it can help the progressive by illuminating some of the emptiness of progressive Christianity.

I don't want to start a war; I seek to build a bridge. While they see us fighting and tearing each other apart, the unbelieving world will have yet another reason not to give the hope of Jesus another hearing. I want to find a way to wrestle with our very real questions in a gracious way and in a way that satisfies our rational minds, all the while sticking with what's solid. I'm convinced that historic Christianity is this solid core. It's the real deal.

People don't stick with historic Christianity simply because they want to and it feels good. Rather, we have been convinced of the truth like Jesus' disciples were. We find ourselves satisfied with no other way than to lay down our lives at the feet of Jesus and ask, "What shall we do to inherit eternal life?" We are convinced that Jesus is worthy and are committed to trying our hardest to live out his commands in the world around us, come what may.

I pray that all of us who claim the name of Christ over ourselves will daily surrender to Jesus through following the teachings he left us in his Word. I know that there are legitimate questions about where we got the Bible. You should ask those questions. A friend of mine once rolled his eyes when I was questioning the origins of the Bible, to which I responded, "Don't you wanna know that these texts you're basing your life decisions on were *really* written down by whom they claim to be written down by?"

To me, that's a very important question. If you're going to forego worldly pleasures in order to follow commands that mostly don't sit well with human nature, shouldn't you want to make sure they're legit? It made sense to me.

But if we're just going with what we feel, we'll end up as Ephesians 4:14 (NLT) describes: "tossed and blown about by every wind of new teaching…influenced when people try to trick us with lies so clever they sound like the truth." Now, I can look back at where I went wrong with Paul and where I ended up as a result. I hope to save some of you from making the same mistake. It's all connected that way. Once you deconstruct one pillar of truth, it becomes easier and easier to take the whole structure down.

MY NEED TO CONTROL

I mentioned earlier that Rob Bell in his book *Velvet Elvis* encouraged everyone to have a trampoline faith versus a brick-wall faith. My question for someone who has deconstructed would be this: If your trampoline has only two springs left on it on opposite sides and you can't really jump on it anymore, but you can still lie on it—is that really still considered a trampoline?

Look at the things you believe. If you no longer believe Jesus literally rose from the dead, and you no longer trust or follow the majority of the Bible, and the way you live/act/breathe in the world looks nothing like what the life of Jesus or his disciples actually looked like—are you really still within bounds to call yourself a Christian (a "little Christ")?

You may wonder why I'm sounding so judgmental right now, and that's fair. But I am not pointing fingers at anyone and saying to trust me because I naturally know the right path to travel. In fact, none of this stuff on my way back from progressivism "felt" right. It all felt backwards from what I thought was the right way. But I gave God and his Word the benefit of the doubt again, and I believe that's the kind of obedience that God longs for from his children. Not ignorantly following, but mostly-informed, fully-trusting kind of following.

That kind of "next right thing" language is actually from somewhere other than Frozen 2 (but thank you for the lovely song, Princess Anna). It comes from recovery programs. I revealed to you earlier that I am, in fact, a sinner and I have struggled with an addiction to pornography. What I haven't revealed to you yet is that my wife of thirteen years, Summer, used to struggle with an addiction to alcohol (yeah, we were a real duo before we both got sober).

She is currently ten years sober, and I am so proud of the woman she has become by following and obeying the Lord's direction in her own life. God has completely restored our marriage in a miraculous way, and we often talk about and thank God for intervening in our story the way he did and for using us as an example of hope for others.

It's funny how God does that. It was around 2014 when my wife was in the process of getting sober and I was in the blissful state of denying I had a porn problem. I visited her one day in rehab for a family day. The teacher had a specific exercise for them to do, and she invited each patient to write on the whiteboard the top five things they were worried would make them relapse once they were out of rehab. My wife, bless her soul, very boldly wrote "My husband" on the top of her list.

When I saw that, my blood began to boil. I had been miserable living with the unpredictability of an alcoholic (all the while ignoring my own sin), yet I stuck around because deep down I loved her and knew it was the right thing to do. How could *I* be reason #1? Wasn't I the reason she was getting sober?? Yet I hid my feelings from her while she explained—and I'm so glad I did. She explained to me that I had always tried to control her every move and never let her just be herself, and that was a big reason she kept drinking.

HOW COULD I BE REASON #1?

So, spoiler alert: Bruce Willis is dead the whole time. If you haven't seen the ending of *The Sixth Sense,* please don't read that previous sentence....You know the part where he's realizing he's dead and the scene just keeps bending out of shape? Yeah...that moment where my wife revealed to me that I was controlling? That was *my* sixth sense moment. My lifelong issues with control flashed before my eyes and the rehab room began to feel like the inside of a lava lamp.

I thought of the first band I was in with my brother and our friend. They both quit at the same time because this little runt (hi, I'm talking about me here) kept trying to tell them how to play their instruments better. I thought of previous girlfriends sitting in the front seat of my car receiving looks of disdain from me when I was disappointed they had hung out with their friends instead of me. I thought of my poor wife longing to have a small part of life out from under my shadow and me making her feel horrible for it. I thought of the fact that, since I had discovered porn at the age of twelve, I had never gone very long without looking at it and yet telling the Lord I would "never do it again."

Most people go into recovery for the surface problem, the addiction, and then find out that they were just using their addiction to cover up some character defect deep down, hidden from themselves. I came to recovery the exact opposite way—by learning about my character defect from the mouth of my sweet, recovering alcoholic wife and then realizing why I had never been able to stop looking at porn: control.

I looked up porn addiction recovery groups online and found a thing called Sexaholics Anonymous. There was a meeting a few blocks from my apartment, so I went. I was shaking when I got out of my car and walked downstairs to the meeting. With a label like "sexaholic," I was expecting to find a bunch of sick freaks down in the basement (dungeon) of that church. But what I found instead was a room full of mirrors.

One person was a reflection of where I'd be if I didn't get sober in ten years, another person was a glimpse of myself in twenty, and so on. These people had lost it all: marriages, respect from their children, freedom, jobs, etc. It literally scared me so much that

I have never been the same since. I'm telling you this for many reasons but for one in particular: Anonymous groups were the place where I learned a new name for God: Higher Power.

BETRAYED BY MY FEELINGS

At first, the higher power thing worked for me. I had some church baggage (see previous chapters) and still saw myself as a "progressive," and the process helped me to disassociate with some of the unhelpful "Christianese." I also did something I heard about that might help me unplug: I stopped reading my Bible and/or things about the Bible for six months. I replaced Bible reading time with prayer time. At the time, I could not read the Bible or understand its teachings without seeing everything through the lens I had been given by my fundamentalist upbringing. The hellfire-and brimstone lens. The *shame-on-you* lens. The God-probably-hates-you-in-real-life lens. I needed to take a break, so I did. Right or wrong, at least I was being honest with God and myself about where I was on the journey.

I always tell people to bring their doubts and questions before God and wrestle with them in his presence. He can absolutely handle it. It's

> **I ALWAYS TELL PEOPLE TO BRING THEIR DOUBTS AND QUESTIONS BEFORE GOD.**

ourselves we should worry about. We may walk away limping. My church's lead pastor says, "If you ever have to choose between the truth or Jesus…choose the truth because it will always lead you back to Jesus." Charles Williams (an old friend of C. S. Lewis) used to say something like, "If there was a question so hard that it could cause Christianity to crumble then it wasn't the truth after all." And so I brought my real self, warts and all, as they say, before the Lord. You can't start at any other place than where you are.

This time with the Lord was sweet. For the first time, I felt like my Father in heaven wasn't disappointed in me. In fact, what I felt from him was delight. The Lord of heaven was looking at me and…smiling (the same way he looks with pleasure on all his creation). I was introduced to the practice of silence and solitude coupled with prayer as a way to fight anxiety (a practice I still do to this day).

The problem is that, over the time of being disconnected from his Word, I began to have thoughts and feelings about God's character that, looking back now, were contradictory to what he says about himself in his Word. I started believing that God looked past my sin because he wanted me to be more focused on loving people. So, I figured, it didn't really matter if I sinned as long as my heart was in the right place (whatever that means!).

During this season, I eventually did come back to the Bible, but by that time I had decided that it was much healthier for me to hold everything I thought I knew about God a little looser than before. Besides, thinking I had it all figured out made me feel judgmental and hypocritical—so that can't be good, right? I had also come to believe that the Bible was written by humans (which it is) and that it was first and foremost a collection of books about man's thoughts about God (which it is not).

It's easy to explain violence in the Old Testament with that hermeneutic, by the way. That way of thinking is also dangerous in explaining away the divine purpose for why Jesus died and what he accomplished on our behalf when he came back from the dead. That hermeneutic makes the Bible a book that can be seen as helpful but not always true or applicable in today's age. I think that hermeneutical shift is actually a sneaky trick of the devil. Taking tips from the *Screwtape Letters:* demons are much more effective at diverting Christians not by jumping out of the shadows and revealing the spiritual realm, but by subtly planting a tiny seed of doubt deep in our consciousness, a seed that grows into seeing the Bible as ridiculous.

The scary fact of the matter is that I was happy when I was not reading my Bible. I *felt* closer to the Lord than ever before and there was way less pressure to do any of the religious stuff I felt guilty for *not* doing when I was younger. I just wanted to simply be. And then when I read the Bible again, the God I thought I knew didn't really look anything like the God of the Bible.

And that is actually my point for this particular chapter. We all have feelings. We have them about anything and everything. They're not inherently good or bad; they're just feelings. But when we take those emotions and put them in the driver's seat, we will end up windblown to far and distant lands with little to no substance to root us in truth.

I had a choice to make: I could either follow my own thoughts and feelings about God *or* I could take a book that claims to be from God and listen to what God says about himself. And that's the fork in the road for every single human being in history. Who is king in your life? Is it your kids? Is it your dream? Is it your secret sin? Is it your thoughts and feelings? Is it you? Or is it the Jesus we find in this ancient book handed down from generation to generation claiming to be *the* truth, with a track record of turning lives around and bringing heaven down to earth one human at a time? That's my choice and that's yours.

THE PRAYER I PRAYED

So, there I was in our baby room holding my first child, wrestling with his future and mine. I wasn't sure what I was going to teach him about God. At the time, I resolved that I could just let my son figure it out. God was big enough to help him. But something dawned in my heart that night that would eventually change my direction and the direction of my family completely: I was beginning to be uncomfortable with the fact that after years of reading progressive books and blogs, listening to podcasts, and late-night convos, *I had nothing concrete.* There was nothing real to hold on to.

Progressive Christianity seemed to be whatever you shaped it to be, and that looked different for each person. It seemed to be a way of poking, prodding, and tearing down rather than of healing and building up. It was a winding detour that led back to the fork in the road I was heading toward in the beginning: to stay within Christianity or leave.

A few weeks went by, as I continued to roll this thought around in my head. Eventually I ended up on my back porch on a sunny spring day. My eyes were closed, and a small stream of smoke was trailing up from the pipe in my hand. I was done being okay with not having any answers. I desperately wanted to know the truth for myself and also for my son and future kids.

I prayed a prayer that I honestly believe changed everything. I asked God to show me the truth. I told him I didn't care where I ended up: Buddhist, Muslim, Mystic. Keeping appearances didn't matter anymore; I just had to know. And after all the searching, after all the thinking, talking, listening, after the changing in my thoughts and feelings, after all the shifting of my childhood beliefs—I was completely shocked and pleasantly surprised when, through the course of a couple years, God gently took me by the hand and led me straight back to the historical Jesus.

QUESTIONS FOR DISCUSSION AND REFLECTION

1. God's grace is indescribably big, unending, and never failing. Describe the moment you realized this and that it was for you.

2. What makes it hard to accept the fact that God delights in you?

3. How would you answer if a child asked you out of curiosity, "Why did Jesus have to die?"

4. Why is it dangerous to dismiss parts of the Bible as non-authoritative because they don't fit our cultural sensibilities? When have you done that?

5. Describe a time in your life when you had to choose whether to do what was right according to Scripture or to do what felt good. How have those decisions gotten easier or more challenging over time?

6. Have you ever struggled (or are you currently struggling) with doubt about God or your salvation? Share that with someone who will pray for you, and take time to encourage each other.

7
THE TOUGH QUESTIONS

I've been asking myself a certain question about my decision-making skills on this next part of my spiritual journey. You'd think that after experiencing Christian music burnout and spending time in a version of Christianity that didn't line up with the historical version, that I wouldn't go back to a conservative church where I could lead people in worship on Sundays. But that's sort of exactly what I did. I asked my best friend his perspective of what he saw me do during that season because I didn't wanna sugarcoat it in my mind to make it sound better.

He plainly said, "You have experienced a lot of real transformation at Harpeth that has been amazing…but you initially took that job because you needed money." Well, there you have it. Thank God for true friends that know you well enough to let you know you're not really the saint you've worked yourself up to be in your mind. So here goes this part of the story, and I'll try to keep it real. The good, the bad, and the shallow.

WHAT NOW?

After Wavorly, I spent a few years touring with one of my all-time favorite Christian bands from my childhood (Audio Adrenaline). These were years when discontent was starting to form in my progressivism, a discontent that magnified at the birth of our firstborn, Bear. Two years after Bear's birth, I realized it was time to come off the road and turn my attention to the family. I faced the harsh reality a lot of musicians who come off the road have to face: what the heck am I gonna do to make money now??

Sure, the road seems glamorous from the outside, but it's difficult on the inside. And some of us were left empty-handed at the end of that road. No real-world skills to transfer over to a real job means no real money to transfer into that bank account. On one of my early job applications under marketing experience, I put, "I ran a merch table?"

People romanticize the idea of touring, like they used to do with running away to join the carnival. I think both carnies and touries have just about the same amount of crazy in our brains and possibly the same number of weekly showers. When you start touring, you really just hit pause on your life and while you're having a lot of fun chasing this dream, your friends from back home are starting careers, buying houses, getting married, and having babies—all awesome, godly things.

SAYING GOODBYE TO TOURING

Now, let me be clear: I absolutely loved my early touring days. It was just me, my best friends in the world, and the road. I think in general our dreams continue to grow bigger as success grows bigger, so we never really feel like we've arrived. But I can honestly say that my original dream actually came true and I'm pretty dang grateful for that.

But, as with any career you choose, reality ends up being different than you imagined. I would often spend five to eight hours a day of driving or riding in a van doing absolutely nothing (this was before iPhones, if you can imagine it). I should've used that time to do something constructive like finishing a bachelor's degree, but instead my bandmates and I usually made up and acted out stupid characters to make each other laugh, like Vampires of the South (look it up).

REALITY ENDS UP BEING DIFFERENT THAN YOU IMAGINED.

At the same time, I really missed getting to do fun stuff and get-togethers with my family back home. I really, really missed my girlfriend and wanted to marry her, but I was so freaking poor! Thus, over several years, my dream had started to turn into a little bit of a nightmare. But I didn't really know how to say that to everyone back home who thought I had "made it." So I ended up sort of "pot committed" and kept pushing forward when really I was just treading water, trying not to drown while everyone I cared about watched.

Then after my girlfriend and I were finally able to get married, having my first child was the straw that broke the camel's back when it came to the "fun" part of touring. I would leave for four days every week and come home to a different-looking baby than when I left. He was changing so fast, and I was missing something important that I'd never get back. I had experienced so much joy and fulfillment from touring, but fatherhood was new and exciting. So, I decided at 34 that my touring days were done.

WORSHIP LEADING?

Being home was quite freeing, but fear also kicked in pretty quickly. The "no real-world skills" was really real all of a sudden. My wife and I had a conversation and decided that, since I wasn't planning on touring anymore and we were working normal jobs, it might be a good idea to move back home to the Southland to be closer to family.

After sharing the news with a few Nashville friends, they kindly but firmly responded, "Yeah, that's not happening." They began to search for people that would hire me in connection to my music and, although I was ready to hang my music career up for good, I had an opportunity to lead worship at a church close to my home in Franklin.

I met with the teaching pastor, Josh. I don't know why, but I felt as if I could tell him everything right away. I immediately opened up with him about my struggles with pornography and my nearly-failed marriage at the time. I felt safe with him, but I never, ever wanted to be a worship leader, so I sort of had nothing to lose. In fact, I felt like leading worship was a giant step backward for me (boy, was I wrong).

I definitely knew I did not want to get hired at a church with the leadership thinking I was this cookie-cutter Christian, and so part of me was trying to push the opportunity away before they got to know the real me (the one who swore, occasionally drank too much, had a problem with lust, and had some major doubts about the Bible—remember, I was still a progressive but praying that God would show me the truth). People have had enough with the "pastor's secret sins exposed!" headlines, and they definitely didn't need another one featuring yours truly.

But to my surprise, Josh went back to the lead pastor of the church and said, "This is our guy!"

That amazing man, Josh, is with Jesus now, and the fact that he followed the whisper of the Spirit that told him I was supposed to be their worship leader still blows my mind. That decision literally changed the trajectory of my life and my family.

TWO WELL-PLACED QUESTIONS

They called me back and set up a second meeting, this time with the head honcho: the lead pastor. So Bobby, Josh, my wife, and I sat down for lunch at Chuy's (do not recommend) and began chatting. I got the feeling that these men were good dudes, but I guessed they were most likely extremely conservative and would be turned off by me (and I was wrong about those two presumptions). I decided I wanted to stick with the theme of authenticity, so I shared with Bobby that I loved reading theology books. He was curious and asked me my favorite authors, and then I dropped a genuine cuss word in conservative church circles: I said I liked reading (cover your eyes) Rob Bell. I thought I might shock him with that answer, but he remained curious without any perceived judgment, so I listed other authors like Francis Chan and Matt Chandler to let him know I was at a place in my life where I wanted to read both sides of arguments and then decide what's true.

Bobby asked me two questions that day and one of them haunted me for weeks after he said it. First, he asked if I was teachable. Ever since I prayed the earnest prayer for God to "show me the truth," that's exactly what I wanted to be. So I said yes.

The second question was the bomb that blew up the path I was on and forced me down a different path, one of uncomfortable but necessary reflection. He said, "Are you willing to be open-minded?" I laughed and simply said, "Yes." But internally I thought, "Of course I'm open-minded; I said I read Rob Bell!" But then he pressed in further by asking, "Are you open-minded about the Bible?"

ARE YOU WILLING TO BE OPEN-MINDED?

Those words echoed in my brain for a few seconds that felt like several minutes. I realized at that moment how I had opened myself up to other new interpretations and revelations *about* the Bible but had in turn closed off my thinking to the historic view *of* the Bible. I was no longer willing to entertain the idea that historic Christianity was the real deal even if it had convincing evidence. That was a real problem for me. I had created my identity around being open and humble with all things. I found comfort in being a guy who didn't have all the answers: a seeker. But somewhere along the way, unbeknownst to myself, I had made up my mind not to give historic Christianity the benefit of the doubt anymore.

WHY WASN'T I OPEN TO HISTORIC CHRISTIANITY?

The bigger question was why. Why had I completely closed myself off to the possibility that the historic Christianity that my first home church tried its best to give me could be true? I needed to find out.

You see, I'm the type of person that needs to understand things before I can move forward. I feel anxious about something until I can understand it, and I believe God gave me that kind of brain for a reason. I feel like one of the main reasons I first began to walk away from Christianity was that the prescription I got for dealing with doubt was to shut down that part of my brain and simply believe more, pray harder, muster up some faith to keep going, and ignore my gut. The Bible says the heart is deceitful among all things, but I don't believe all intuitions we have are wrong when something's gone sideways. I think those feelings can be red flags for the state of our hearts and that it's important to stop and ask why we're feeling that way and process it openly with a trusted Christ follower.

So, I guess you could say I reached a new level in my deconstruction: I was ready to deconstruct…my deconstruction. I was completely intrigued by Bobby's tough question, and I just had to find out what this "conservative" pastor meant by being open-minded. I was interested in going down the rabbit hole. Maybe I missed something the last time I was down there. So, when they asked me to start a trial period of leading worship at their church, I took the job.

Side note: Personally, I don't think it's wise to suggest to someone, "Whatever you do, DON'T deconstruct!" Deconstruction, in my experience, is something that can just spring up and happen to you. It's like grief or a loss. It's there, it's reality. Now what are you going to do with it? You can either ignore it and let it eventually consume you, or you can take the Father's hand and let him lead you through the doubts and questions. He knows the way through the maze.

I believe you have to be real with God, as well as with a trusted follower of Jesus, about all the doubts and all the questions. You have to bring it before God and ask him to help you understand. He desires a real relationship with you and when you're hiding there's no chance for that. He already knows what you're thinking anyway. No need for leafy bikinis and speedos like our ancestors; come on out and bare it all. Peace most certainly won't happen overnight, but little by little, as you grapple with these questions one at a time, you will begin to feel lighter, and you will be able to trust the God of the Bible again. The only way out is through. And once you get to the other side, you've reached the most important part of this journey: the reconstruction.

RECONSTRUCTING WELL

Everyone who deconstructs reconstructs into something. The important thing is to reconstruct well. Don't reconstruct in a vacuum with Google as your guide, and definitely don't succumb to the dreaded TikTok theology. Your algorithm has been set to give you the most relatable answer to what you've already been thinking. You need someone older than you who 1) knows the Bible, 2) actually tries their best to follow it, and 3) is a safe, nonjudgmental person.

You may be thinking those people don't exist. Trust me, they do. They're often the quiet ones because they have nothing to prove and they know that God is the one in charge. No need to be the loudest voice in the room when you're at peace internally like that. If you can't find somebody like that, pray for that somebody to find you. It is God's will for you that you would be a real disciple of Jesus. Do you know what happens when our prayers completely sync up with God's will? Things happen. Pray, trust, keep your eyes open and keep processing these doubts and questions openly with the Holy Spirit.

I wonder if the reason we're seeing a huge falling away from the faith right now is that people are either reconstructing in total isolation from embarrassment or, worse, reconstructing with a false sense of community on social media that just echoes their doubts and questions with no real solutions. I understand that it can feel good. There are some hilarious TikTok vids that poke at the church, and let's be honest: there are Christians that spoon-feed these content creators pure golden material to make those videos. But I would like to help people move on from that phase of deconstruction.

What about the "I'm openly questioning my faith and what I need more than answers right now is to hear people say 'me too'" phase? Many get to that point (especially today), but it's not good to stay there. Seeing people stuck there now makes me a little sad. I long to see people develop and grow and move forward in life.

I want to see them take risks and fall flat and learn a huge lesson and then get back up again. That's living.

Sitting contently in your doubts and questions is not living and it's not faith. But *wrestling* with them is. Wrestling with your doubts and questions is hard work and wears you out, and to me, that's a sign of genuine faith. If someone is taking seriously the things of God, oh my gosh, there's hope. If you're reading this and you're fine with your doubts and questions, but you've never moved toward solutions *with* God's guidance, then you're stuck. I hope you will hit your knees in your room tonight and pray that prayer that I prayed long ago and mean it: "God, I don't care where it takes me or who I become as a result. I have to know the truth. Will you show me?" Pray that and see what the Lord of Heaven and Earth will do to open your eyes and give you real peace and joy beyond your wildest dreams. Do it.

A MENTOR AND FRIEND

Okay, back to my reconstruction. My lead pastor Bobby plays a prominent role in the rest of this story. I told you earlier that I never wanted to be a worship leader, but God had a much bigger plan for me than I ever could've made up myself. Bobby discipled me so well, and part of the reason why I wanted to start writing this book was to document his process because it worked for me. And it just might work with the lost and wandering people in your life.

So here goes. First, Bobby wanted to be my friend, and that's a crucial part of any discipling relationship: authentic connection. When my mentor realized God wanted him to start discipling me, he sought after me. He called me—sometimes daily. He invited me over to his house. He invited himself over to my house (which could've been awkward, but he did these things to make our relationship as easy as it could be for me).

You have to be intentional with whomever you're discipling and sometimes it takes hard work to get the relationship started in the beginning. He brought me to hockey games. He took my family out to lunch after church. He asked me to join his home group. All of this was a way of creating organic context for intentional conversation. Let me say that again in a less churchy way: he set up frequent hang out times to build rapport with me so that I would lower my walls and be enough of the real me around him—all with the goal in mind of finding a way to begin speaking *into* me and calling the good *out of* me.

> **SOMETIMES IT TAKES HARD WORK TO GET THE RELATIONSHIP STARTED IN THE BEGINNING.**

We became real friends, and looking back I really enjoyed that time. Whenever we were in the car on the way to watch the Preds play, we would "naturally" talk about theology, and when he heard me share something that I believed, his response was always curiosity—even when something I believed was maybe a little off from what the Bible teaches. Bobby knows the Bible very well, so when moments like that came up, he would ask me to open up my Bible app and we would read what the text said together.

This was not awkward; it was just what we did. He would then ask me, "What is the author of that book saying?" Notice he didn't ask, "What does that passage mean to *you*?" That question would have been what I was used to answering in my many theological conversations that were leading me away from the truth in the Bible and toward the "truth" that I felt was right. You can't wiggle around what the author means, but you can wiggle around what you think or what you want it to say, for sure. "What is the author saying?" removes the wiggle-room right out of there.

WHO WOULD KNOW BETTER?

There was another phrase Bobby used boldly that would sort of shock me back to reality. Whenever certain topics would come up and he would sense a distrust in me toward the Bible and a preference to lean on modern thought *about* the Bible, Bobby would simply say, "Well, who would better know what Jesus meant than the men that were actually with him?" I felt a little embarrassed the first time he asked me. This was because a lot of my personal theology was built on what 20th- and 21st-century white progressives had to say about what they *thought* Jesus meant versus what the apostles *knew* he meant, because Jesus had explained it to them himself. Progressive authors base theology on the things Jesus "could have meant" while the apostles explained the things they knew he meant.

Bobby also did a great job of bringing these real men in the Bible (and also the very real nation of Israel) back to life in my mind. He's sort of a fanatic for archaeological evidence that's been discovered over the last couple centuries, and this evidence actually props up what the Bible describes. In countless cases, archaeologists have found the geography of that region to be exactly as the Bible says it should be as it's written down in Scripture. And when it doesn't exactly line up, simply wait a few years or decades and they'll usually discover a missing piece that ends up proving what the Bible has described all along; we simply hadn't dug up enough of the equation just yet.

Bobby also walked me through the criteria that had to be met in order for the books and letters that eventually made it into the canon to be considered divine Scripture. First, he showed me how the books that were to be considered holy and inspired were not originally decided on by a faculty of men who sought to prop up a narrative about Jesus in order to push for their own agendas (that's the narrative Progressive Christianity gave me). Rather, these letters were already being viewed and treated as holy and inspired by the first churches started by the apostles. The letters that became our Bible had to either be written by the apostles themselves or by men closely related to and discipled by the apostles, and each letter or book had to line up with the others theologically.

NOT WANTING TO BELIEVE VS. EXPLORING THE EVIDENCE

Bobby helped me get acquainted with the real people who scribed the New Testament, of whom Luke is probably my favorite. I didn't know he was a physician who followed Paul around and is still highly respected as an ultra-thorough historian by modern historians today. This was a huge moment in reestablishing my trust in the Bible. I couldn't trust sleazy, agenda-pushing men, reclining in their chairs, smoking stogies, and deciding what was in the Bible and what was out, but I could trust a well-respected historian who has been proven right time and time again when tested historically and geographically.

The evidence that supports the Bible being true is overwhelming. To ignore that, some part of you (probably a subconscious part) has to want to disbelieve parts of the Bible because it is hard to look at the world through the lens of the Bible. And I think it's likely that's what brings a lot of progressives to where they are now, because that's where I was back then. Sometimes the Bible is black and white on issues that seem to be full of gray in the "real world." When you come to that point in your life where reality is complicated like it is, it creates a hard fork in the road that would be difficult for anyone trying to follow a 2,000-year-old book. When I was making my way back to historic

Christianity, I realized how much of the Bible I simply didn't *want* to believe: its stances on homosexuality, male headship, a literal hell, handling money, etc. But because I had been convinced of the validity and the truth of it, I began giving God the benefit of the doubt.

THE BENEFIT OF THE DOUBT

There's another phrase my mentor used in order to bring me back to the Bible. He said that, when he comes across things in the Bible that don't sit well with him, he gives God the benefit of the doubt instead of just trying to figure out a way to work around it. As an example, after I had come back around on the apostle Paul being legit and someone who wrote with the authority of Christ, I really struggled with the idea of male headship in the church and at home. I got such a weird feeling in my stomach when I read passages like 1 Corinthians 11:2–16 ("The head of the woman is man..."). As a progressive, that gut feeling would guide me to land on a different philosophy on life rather than "Paul's opinion," as I would have described it then.

When it comes to reading through passages like 1 Corinthians 11, a discipling relationship actually becomes *crucial.* In our conversations, Bobby would ask me to read the passage out loud. Then he asked me what the author meant when he wrote it. Then he asked me if I had any questions, to which I responded, "What does he mean by head?" Bobby would walk me through details like that with great patience to help me understand. After we did that, I would go back home still feeling a bit weird about it, but I remembered the phrase "Give God the benefit of the doubt," so that's exactly what I did.

AN EXAMPLE

I am not naturally a leader; I feel most comfortable in background positions. Yet God has consistently placed me in positions of leadership over the years, so I've grown to be comfortable with it. At the time Bobby walked me through the passages about the husband's headship, I was certainly not leading my family. I was being super passive and just going with the flow. I thought that the apostle Paul was encouraging men to "take the power back that was rightfully theirs." But that's not at all the way Jesus led his followers, was it?

Now when I read Paul's writing on male headship, I process it through the lens of Jesus' leadership. That process of understanding (or that hermeneutic principle) is called "letting Scripture interpret Scripture." And what kind of leader was Jesus? He was a *servant* leader; a completely laid-down-his-life leader, not a take-the power-back leader. So that's how I began following that hard teaching in the Bible that on the surface seemed offensive and barbaric to my 21st century Western brain.

I am trying my best to lead my family now, the way I understand God designed marriage to work, and my wife is happy and free to be her whole, real self and live out her dream life of being a stay-at-home mom with lots of animals…and chickens (what a hippie). It wasn't that she was dominating our family and running us off a cliff. She was doing a great job in her role in our family. But in my passivity and fear of being a toxic male, I wasn't really standing up for my wife and kids by being the chief servant in our household.

In fact, even now as I lead my family in what I believe to be a biblical fashion, the "power" is actually not really mine like people might assume it is. I'm not overruling my wife's decision on where to park the car when we go to Target to spend $200 on 3 items. It's much more of a backwards power. I feel as if I have received the "power" to lead by completely laying down my life for my wife and kids.

If that's not a backward definition of male headship from how contemporary culture would define it, I don't know what is. But I've been re-convinced that the Creator of this world knows what he's doing way more than I do, and so though I had my preconceived ideas of what God *probably* meant with this chauvinistic idea of male headship thing, I decided to give him the benefit of the doubt *knowing* that it is not in the character of the Ancient One to be a domineering, oppressive dictator over someone. No, Jesus was the greatest servant of all.

And when I pushed forward in prayer for the changing of my wife's heart and for clarity on what my role would be, I was pleasantly surprised to see that male headship literally meant having a license to be more Christlike, to be more loving and faithful and loyal and more attentive to my wife and children than I was previously as a passive dad or in the way the world views male headship as a dominating, toxic male. Give God the benefit of the doubt, and I promise you'll see that God's way of life is absolutely beautiful and the best thing for us personally and for everyone else around us. The proof of humanity's fall and truth of redemption is all around us if we're willing to take a step of faith and bet that God is all things good and lovely.

YOU DON'T WANT TO LEAVE TOO, DO YOU?

That's actually how this Christian faith works. I grew up thinking that to be a Christian meant to believe in a list of claims about Jesus. He was God's Son, he was perfect, and he died for me and rose again. Boom. Saved. Book of Life and all that. But after reading through the book of Acts several times, I'm convinced that our level of faith is tied directly to our level of obedience to the Holy Spirit and Scripture. And sometimes, we might not feel like obeying until we start obeying. Maybe I should, but most times I don't feel like it.

> OUR LEVEL OF FAITH IS TIED DIRECTLY TO OUR LEVEL OF OBEDIENCE TO THE HOLY SPIRIT AND SCRIPTURE.

What really helped me in my obedience was believing that if anyone knew the best way this world worked and how I'm supposed to find my place in it, it would be the One who created it all. That's the motivation and trust that runs through my mind when I come across hard teachings in Scripture. And let's be honest—there are a lot of those!

Before ending this chapter, I want to highlight one word I said in the previous paragraph: *feel*. In my experience, obedience looks like choosing what you don't feel in order to line up with what God wants for your life. That stuff is hard. I find myself every couple years tripping over something in Scripture. The space between following Jesus and doing what I feel is right can be paper thin. Whenever I'm in that space, I'm reminded of Jesus turning to the Twelve after insisting the crowd eat his flesh and drink his blood and asking, "You do not want to leave me too, do you?" "Simon Peter answered him, "Lord, to whom shall we go? You have the words of eternal life. We have come to believe and to know that you are the Holy One of God" (John 6:67–69).

That's where everyone in humanity fits into the story. We're all standing in the crowd of John 6. There's a man standing in front of us, and his words sound like craziness to some and feel like energy pulsing in the hearts of others. His words have the power to bring gut-wrenching feelings of anger and indignation at the thought of someone asking them to do deeds so seemingly anti-human. But for those of us that know who he is, the One from the beginning, and to know that his words flow back to the origin of time itself, to the way things should be, we know that his words are an ever-flowing river of life. He knows how it should be because everything came about through him and he is the One for whom all of it (including us) was made in the first place.

We're in a moment in history where a person's truth is said to trump all. People are so deeply in touch with their truth (i.e., their feelings) that they're willing to forsake family, friends, and even sound reason to stay true to it. It's odd that our feelings could be the thing that most divides us as people and that potentially paves the way for societal collapse to come. When my feelings + my experience = true truth, regardless of what God says, then all manner of destruction follows.

AN UPSIDE-DOWN WORLD

I love it when my feelings and experiences line up with Scripture. In fact, I feel lucky when that happens. But during this most recent part of my story, I learned the secret that countless other followers of Jesus found out before me: following Scripture and the Spirit is the beginning of a journey of multiple forks in roads where your "gut" overwhelmingly tells you the opposite of what Jesus says, and you have to decide with your mind which way to lean.

And if you're wondering why that's the case, I believe it's because we were born into a fallen world where things were already flipped upside down. People say Jesus has an upside kingdom, but really our world is the one standing on its head since the fall. My point is that we all have feelings and knee-jerk reactions to the gospel. Those are not new. That is a cyclical thing where every generation has to decide what they're going to do.

I challenge you, the next time you come across a place in Scripture that doesn't sit well with you, please do two things: 1) give God the benefit of the doubt that he knows what's best, and 2) obey the teaching before it feels right. And if you have a hard time with that second one, trust me, I understand. That's been a struggle since the first two humans.

But I will warn you of this. If you choose to follow your instinct over Scripture, I do not judge you, but you may wake up one day, several forks in the road later, and feel totally okay with the fact that your life looks way different than it did when you once believed that the Bible contained God's actual words. You may feel good about the fact that your daily decisions don't need to be classified as "sin" because those sin lists were made up by unenlightened people.

But you also may realize that by your choices you have already given a devastating answer to the one question that we all must answer before we leave this world for the next: "You do not want to leave me too, do you?"

QUESTIONS FOR DISCUSSION AND REFLECTION

1. If you currently have an older, wiser, trustworthy Christian in your life that you can share your struggles with, who is it?

If you don't, pray for God to bring someone like this into your life.

2. What's one thing you're wrestling with internally right now about God or the Bible? Be brutally honest.

3. When studying the Bible, how might using the phrase "What is the author saying?" versus "What do you think about that Bible verse?" change the way you understand and apply Scripture to your life?

4. As you study Scripture, what teachings make you feel uncomfortable?

5. As you engage with the Bible, what is a new habit you want to cultivate in order to become a stronger student of God's Word?

6. Are you willing to begin giving God the benefit of the doubt? Meaning, when you come across something in Scripture that doesn't sit well with you, are you willing to sit uncomfortably in that teaching and ask God to show you his heart?

8
THERE AND BACK AGAIN?

My wife and I had an interesting conversation the other day. She asked me, "What do you call yourself when you're talking to people about your faith?" I answered, "I typically describe myself as a 'follower of Jesus' rather than calling myself a 'Christian.'"

I'm not embarrassed by the word "Christian" or anything. I think most of us are aware that the first followers of Jesus referred to themselves as *disciples* while the rest of the world called them "little Christs" (aka *Christians*) as a derogatory term. In some ways, I feel I'm not qualified to call myself a little Christ, but hopefully people would describe me in that way.

But for the part I can control, I wake up every day and choose to follow Jesus with my decisions for that day. I'm a disciple, a student if you will, at the feet of Jesus. I'm learning and applying.

I'm failing—a lot. But I'm being honest about those failures and getting right back up.

I'll also tell people I'm aligned with the historic beliefs of Christianity. What I mean by that is the major beliefs that the first Christians believed.

Before I delve into some specific beliefs, I'd like to talk about how radically my life has changed since coming back to historic Christianity. One of the main differences between the deconstructing me and the reconstructed me is that I no longer identify as a progressive or a spiritual wanderer.

This doesn't mean I'm completely satisfied with every single answer historic Christianity gives me for every question about God and the Bible, but it does mean that I'm more settled in my faith when it comes to those questions. I still don't have the answers to all the tough questions, but they no longer dominate my thinking and certainly don't send me down a years-long trip of doubting and deconstruction anymore. And that's an incredible thing! I was stuck there for so long, and now I finally feel free.

I definitely still hit bumps in the road, but I've got a few tools that I didn't have before:

1. TRANSPARENCY WITH SPIRITUALLY MATURE PEOPLE.

With these people in my life, I can open up to them about the things I'm wondering without judgment, and I still do that from time to time. Questions kept in secret create black holes within our spirits, and they can eventually suck all the life out of us if we're not careful to talk about them with someone. I believe everyone has questions, sometimes soul-crushing ones. The difference is how we deal with them.

While I was deconstructing, I dealt with the questions by stuffing the doubts down. If you've ever tried that, you know that doesn't work for very long. Some people ignore their questions. This creates a blissful yet ignorant state of mind. To me, these people seem like they're white-knuckling their faith while not facing reality. They seem happy enough, but in a sort of creepy way (for example, like everything is hinging on one specific prayer request that they *really* need answered and if they just keep reciting the magical phrases and believing, then everything will turn out just fine).

Don't be that person or any of those types of persons I just listed. Find yourself an open follower of Jesus and, when the speed bumps come up, give them a call and push through the awkwardness and get the

YOU'RE ONLY AS SICK AS YOUR SECRETS.

secret thought out. You will feel a weightlessness about you that you maybe have never felt before. Recovery programs have a truer than true saying that's worth pondering: you're only as sick as your secrets.

2. A QUIET AND PATIENT TRUST IN GOD.

I don't have an urgency for my questions to be answered right away like I did before. I trust the Holy Spirit to lead me in the direction of truth, but sometimes I'm not even close to being ready to hear that truth. So, when I ask God to reveal something to me, I simply wait. When my consciousness is ready to handle the truth (suddenly I'm picturing Jack Nicholson in a courtroom with veins popping out of his forehead), the Holy Spirit will reveal it to me.

This goes back to the "giving God the benefit of the doubt" thing I mentioned earlier. If you trust that he's good, you'll find the ability to chill out and trust him while you wait for an answer to come. You'll find yourself in a state of peace in the not-knowing for now. I suppose you've got a bigger problem on your hands if you don't trust that he's good.

If that's you, and you genuinely want to know if he's actually good, reach out to him with an earnest prayer and ask him to show you that he's good. But keep in mind this probably won't happen if you've already made up your mind. Would you waste time trying to convince someone you're a nice person if you could clearly tell they were never going to believe you?

3. BETTER SOURCES FOR UNDERSTANDING.

I took a brief class on Greek (not enough to understand it all or read it, but enough to understand *some* things about the language). I've also found the Blue Letter Bible app to be a great way to double check meanings and get answers closely linked to how ancient people thought of biblical terms—and not *closely* linked to the way 21st-century progressive thinkers want to interpret the Greek.

I want to know what the author meant and how the audience would've received it, not what a certain word or two *could mean* to any given modern thinker. I'm way less intrigued by the phrase "could have meant" now, where I once was enamored with it. It throws up a red flag for me now. "How is it that after thousands of years of people studying and seeking the things of God, that this North American dude-bro ended up being THE one to crack the code on what Jesus 'actually' meant?" I'm done with that.

SO, WHAT EXACTLY AM I?

These tools have helped me continue on the journey of not identifying as a skeptic or a progressive anymore, although I sometimes jokingly say I'm still a recovering skeptic. Honestly, my default reaction probably always will be a little skepticism, and I don't think that's a bad thing.

I used to feel guilty for that, but a good friend of mine helped me understand that I was probably just created that way. He referred to me as an intellectual (which I immediately laughed at), but he explained that being an intellectual doesn't necessarily mean you're smart. I thought, *Okaaay, keep talking...* He said that intellectuals typically feel anxiety over something they don't understand and won't feel right about a subject until they've studied it. I totally feel that way about a lot of things.

It's funny. That sort of wiring in my brain sent me down the deconstruction path to begin with, but it has also turned out to be one of my greatest strengths on the other side of progressivism. Studying the Word, the commentaries, and doing the research actually help me understand, but doing these also helps me to let go. That may not be how your brain works, and that is totally fine. You might be better off than me, honestly. But if your brain does work that way, a word of encouragement to you: God may have just designed you that way for a reason. It might be a good idea to spend some time praying and fasting for how God may want to use that gift in and through you.

So, I've covered what I wouldn't call myself anymore (skeptic, progressive). But what *would* I call myself now? I've really wrestled with this answer even as I've been writing this chapter. It would be nice to say that "I started out evangelical, went progressive, and came back to evangelicalism." Boom. Wrap it up and put a bow on it....

But that wouldn't really be the whole truth, would it? I guess I've landed in a place *similar* to where I started out, but…different. My eyes have been opened to certain things, and there's no fully going back. Like Bilbo Baggins in *The Hobbit*, I once was safe and secure in the Shire, but I went on an adventure with strange people and I've once again returned to the Shire, but with visible scars and just a tad bit weird. In the book, the neighboring hobbits were a little unsure what to do with the new Bilbo. Or maybe a better example would be Frodo coming back without an index finger and with a huge scar on his chest.

Either way, I couldn't outright say that I'm 100% an evangelical again. What I mean is that I'm a tad bit weird, and—perhaps my fellow hobbits are a little unsure what to do with me! I do love the original meaning of the word "evangelical," as it is based on the word meaning "good news." But as I was saying with the word "Christian" earlier, the definition of "evangelical" seems to have changed over time, if only in the minds of nonbelievers.

The word "evangelical" may even be making you flinch as you read it because you've got some real church hurt by so-called people of the good news. The word "evangelical" may conjure up images of judgmental Christians characterized by their hatred of certain people groups or their allegiance to a certain political party. When most people hear the word "evangelical" now, they don't automatically think "good news." They probably don't think of the word "good" at all, to be honest.

Perhaps the next label that comes to mind is far-right Republican. Fundamentalist. Gay-hating transphobe who votes pro-life in order to control women's bodies. Most people may think evangelicals are stupid and way behind the times.

While I don't believe those things are true of evangelicals, I'm sort of afraid of what happens if I wear the label now, because of what it might bring up in the mind of someone I'm trying to find an "in" with for the gospel. That label can hinder the type of evangelism I'm trying to do.

I'm a slow-burn kind of evangelist; I don't prefer the shouting-through megaphones-on-street-corners method. I don't prefer the handing-out-tracts method like I used to do in college. I prefer the method that was used to slowly melt my heart of stone and get me to look at Jesus again. And if we really take a good look at how Jesus was with his disciples, we'll see it's the exact method he used: life-on-life discipleship. It's subtle, but man is it effective. Jesus took three years with his disciples and look what happened.

> **JESUS TOOK THREE YEARS WITH HIS DISCIPLES AND LOOK WHAT HAPPENED.**

So, I'm fine with labeling myself a disciple of Jesus who tries to line up with historic Christianity, but at this point and time, I feel like there's just too much baggage in the hearts of lost people to proudly claim the label *evangelical* for myself and potentially close off any line of communicating the gospel with those people.

You may not feel that way, and I do understand that. I'm not advocating that you should think like me on this. I try my best to be a person who gives anyone a fair hearing instead of judging their book by its cover, but I know not everyone I will try to reach is like that. And I want every chance I can get for a person to know me before they make judgments on my character based on the label of a people group that may have hurt them in the past. I want a real shot at introducing them to the real Jesus.

MY BELIEFS THEN AND NOW

To bring it around full circle, unlike when I was progressive, I actually believe the good news again. I believe it's real and I want everyone to know it and to surrender their lives to Jesus because it's the best thing for them. *It's the best way to live.* Now, every time I befriend a stranger, I'm thinking in the back of my mind, "How can I help them see Jesus?" I know that makes me sound like a fanatical Christian, but I honestly believe the good news isn't just good…it's the BEST news, so why wouldn't I want people to hear about it??

Contrast that back to when I was progressive: I don't think I actually wanted people to hear the good news because deep down I wasn't so sure I believed it myself anymore. How sad is that? That breaks my heart even writing that out. I didn't want people to hear the very thing that could've turned their lives around....

Here are some other ways my beliefs have settled since leaving progressive Christianity. I went from thinking Jesus probably wasn't aware he was the Messiah to knowing that Jesus definitely knew he was the Son of God. From responses like "I am he" when asked about the Messiah (see John 4:26; Matthew 26:63–64), I think it's plain to see that in Scripture now, but I forgot that when I was progressive. If that's not a case for always staying in the Word, I don't know what is. When you're not in it, you simply begin to forget it.

I used to question why Jesus had to die. I suspected that the Christian answer "it pleased God" lined up with the progressive answer that it was "cosmic child abuse." (How do they come up with such catchy, deceptive phrases??) My thinking at the time was that the cross might very well have been "child abuse" because, since God had the end in mind when he created the world, he must have planned to severely punish his Son all along, right? Well, if it weren't for those words Jesus said in the garden (Matthew 26:36–42), then maybe, but Jesus literally said he was willingly laying down his life (John 10:17–18). I'm confident now that the reason Jesus died was to save the world from the wrath of God, according to dozens of Old Testament prophecies and direct words from Jesus himself.

I used to wonder if Jesus *literally* rose from the grave or just *metaphorically* rose in spirit—a sort of "carrying on of the torch" by his disciples. (By the way, I'm now rolling my eyes at myself for believing that one, so feel free to do the same.) Now I would say I'm as confident as you can be without having been there that Jesus physically came back to life after defeating sin and death. Yes, I'm confident because of what the scriptures say, but also because the earliest attempt to explain away the resurrection (that the disciples came and stole Jesus' body) assumed that they never found Jesus' body. The religious leaders that hated him and sent him to the cross were paranoid that the disciples were going to steal his body so they doubled up on security—and then ended up spreading the rumor that Jesus' disciples *did* steal the body, even though the disciples wouldn't have had that ability. *Something* obviously happened back then, something that caused a stir, and the most logical explanation would be that Jesus did what these historically and geographically accurate eyewitness accounts say he did: rose from the dead.

I went from believing the Bible was a collection of stories from humans *about* God to believing how Jesus himself viewed and treated Scripture: as God's word written *through* the hands of humans by the power of the Holy Spirit. This is how Christians throughout all time have handled the Bible. Cultures are cyclical. Just because Scripture goes against the grain of *our* culture doesn't mean we ought to do away with certain verses in the Bible. I'm sure there were plenty of things going on back then that didn't line up with Scripture. I mean…Christians throughout history have been persecuted and murdered because of Scripture. It's never going to fit in a fallen world.

I went from thinking large portions of the Bible were wrong to believing that the Bible is inerrant (while not always maximally precise).

I went from thinking there was no hell and that everyone (eventually) would end up in heaven, to aligning my thoughts with the only one to ever go there and see for himself. Jesus says there is an afterlife where people go—either to one of the worst places imaginable or to a place greater than the fanciest things you've ever seen called *heaven,* where he (the Messiah) is seated on the throne.

I used to think the people of God would bring about utopia one policy at a time to the point where the world was good enough on its own. That point would, in a way, be heaven. But now I agree with the one who was here when everything was set in motion at the beginning of time, and he says that history will culminate in the day when he comes back to judge the living and the dead and restore all things.

By the way, this is me finally getting down to the nitty-gritty—to the differences between progressive Christianity and historic Christianity. It feels a little weird to juxtapose the two lines of thinking like that. But I will say as I'm ending this book, as I look back on my own story, I do sort of feel like my life has been split into three sections, and I've taken something with me in each third part of my journey.

THREE STAGES IN THE JOURNEY

When I was an evangelical in the first third of my journey, I witnessed to people. All. The. Time. Gas station clerks. Mission trips to Bourbon Street in New Orleans. Wherever I went, we were evangelizing people all the time. But I didn't really *care* about the people—not really. I mostly got sad when someone rejected the "How to Get to Heaven" tract I was offering because I wanted my Baptist Student Union Director to be proud that I "saved" someone. That's such a backwards reason for doing that, but that's the truth.

> **I DIDN'T REALLY CARE ABOUT THE PEOPLE— NOT REALLY.**

But in the second third of my journey, when I was a progressive, I learned how to actually care about people. I got into the lives of "sinners" from all walks of life. I sat down with the alcoholic. I slept on the floor of houses with marriages barely hanging on by a thread. I listened to the gut-wrenching stories of bullying from the pasts of LGBTQ+ people. My heart broke for these people, but I never gave them a good answer. I just listened, which is good but only half the battle.

I see it now, in the final third of my journey. Jesus is the answer. He's the best thing there is. It's all about him, and we get the chance to know him and it's unbelievably rich and good. I'm ashamed of myself for being someone so wrapped up in legalism in my first third that I couldn't see the poor sinner in front of me. I'm also ashamed of myself for partaking in drunkenness and debauchery in my second third, all the while having the precious jewel of life locked secretly away in my heart. I'm looking through tears as I'm writing this for all the wasted opportunities and time with people whom I will never have the chance to talk with so intimately again, that may end up separated from God forever at the end. I don't ever want to squander my time like that again.

What I'm trying to apply in this third part is both the richness of the truth that my upbringing taught me by keeping my nose in the Bible *with* the wonder and the mystery of the grace that has been shown to me by Jesus who eats with sinners. I seek to live every single day with the conviction of the truth in all of Scripture and *with* a heart full of grace and compassion for the broken world right in front of me.

We have been given the best deal of our lives, people. Really. We were nothing. Nobodies. And the greatest person to have ever lived looked at you and he looked at me with tears in his eyes and he said, "I can help them."

And now we're free. Let's be the kind of people who know him so well that there's no question of who we are. That no one would look at you and say, "Oh he's an evangelical; you can tell because he hates gay people." But rather that people would say, "That person is unlike any other person I've ever met. They're so kind and caring." Why? Because the character of Jesus is so much upon you that the you that was there before, the one with all the baggage, with all the hurt, with all the doubts and the anger, the one with all the hidden sin, isn't defining you anymore. The real you is the gracious character of Jesus that looks at the world and says through you, "Here I am. I can help."

That's the person I seek to be now after this there-and-back-again trip through deconstruction, progressivism, reconstruction, and finally peace in the here and now. I don't know where you are in your journey, but please let what you've read here fill you with hope that, whatever part you're on right now, there is a hand that will carry you through. And it's the same hand that made you and knows you and loves you forever. Amen.

QUESTIONS FOR DISCUSSION AND REFLECTION

1. Is there a follower of Christ that you are regularly transparent with? If not, pray about who that could be, and pray that you can be courageous enough to ask that person to be in a transparent relationship with you.
2. Describe a time where you had to be patient in waiting for the Lord.
3. What resources do you use for questions about God or the Bible? List books, websites, apps, etc. How can you vet those out to determine if they are representing the true Word of God?
4. Describe an experience with the Lord that has been life-altering.

5. Do you *really* believe the gospel is true? Do you believe it's true in your life? Why or why not?

6. As Christ followers, we are called to be full of grace and truth. What are some things you can begin this week to help you be full of both?

CONCLUDING THOUGHTS

Thank you so much for reading my book. It means a lot to me that you took time to walk around in my head and shoes for a little while. In wrapping up, I'd like to send you some encouragements as you continue down the path you're on with the Lord.

FIRST, TO THOSE WHO'VE NEVER DOUBTED:

I am the prodigal son who returned, and you are my brother who stayed and kept the faith. That's amazing, and I'm genuinely happy for you. How are you doing? And what does keeping the faith actually mean? A quick search online will tell you that faith is the "complete trust or confidence in someone or something." It also means conviction. Belief. Confidence.

I love the way my church describes the word. They taught me that, looking closely at the Greek word for faith we find in Scripture (*pistis*), it means something more like a *faithful* faith,

LOSING MY FAITH ... IN PROGRESSIVE CHRISTIANITY

an ongoing faithful life. I grew up thinking faith meant merely believing. I specifically thought it meant believing a list of things *about* Jesus. But when we look at Scripture, we see people placing a *faithful* faith in Jesus that brings them to the point of obeying his commands in an ongoing way. That's different than just believing he existed and was the Son of God and all that.

In the culture I grew up in, it was considered honorable to white knuckle things and keep believing and never doubt. For me, it was either I was saved and a good Christian because I *knew* that I believed, or I was feeling tremendous anxiety because I was having trouble believing. If you haven't had those anxious seasons of doubt and don't have trouble believing, maybe you're feeling pretty good about yourself. But again, faith isn't just about believing the right things, but about living an ongoing, obedient faith in Jesus as king. I'd encourage you to ask yourself this question: *Am I pursuing a faithful faith in Jesus, or am I holding on to a date and time or a certificate, taking pride in something I did way back when?* Could there be some hidden pride that you never released? Could there even be secret resentment that your prodigal brothers and sisters get a welcome home party when you're the one who never left?

AM I PURSUING A FAITHFUL FAITH IN JESUS?

Remember these words from Jesus' story: "'My son,' the father said, 'you are always with me, and everything I have is yours.'" Be at peace, as together, we respond to our Father's forever faithfulness with a faithful faith.

TO THOSE STILL STRUGGLING UNDER THE WEIGHT OF DOUBT:

You are going to make it through this. Write down "This too shall pass" on a Post-it and stick it to your mirror so you see it every day. What you're going through is like a bout of depression, but it won't be like this forever. Don't turn back to look at your old, pre-Jesus life and let your faith turn into a useless pillar of salt. Keep pressing forward and let God take your scars and turn them into stories to be shared with others going through the same thing. Let your wounds become badges of grace as you see people set free by hearing your testimony.

Get some exercise to get out of your head. I once heard an ex-drug addict freed by Christ say, "Whenever I'm lost in my own head, I hop in the truck and search for someone to help. Pulls me right back out." Do that. Keep telling God how you're feeling and allow him to enter into the sadness with you. The worst thing you can do is distrust the One who knows you and formed you and understands you more than anyone else. Give God the benefit of the doubt and wait for him to show you his goodness again. Trust me, he will.

TO THOSE WHO WANT TO HELP THEIR DECONSTRUCTING FRIENDS:

I'm in this fight with you. Let's pray and fast for our friends that are deconstructing, or have left the faith, and ask God to open their eyes and melt their hearts of stone. Let's pray hard against our common enemy who has confused them and command him in the name of the Lord Jesus to leave them alone. Let's go to spiritual battle for our loved ones and do the hard work of keeping the faith that God hears those prayers and has a heart for our friends too (even bigger than our own hearts for them).

Join me in studying the scriptures, learning the art of apologetics, and becoming good listeners, all with the intention of nurturing safe spaces for open conversations about God. And as we wait for the Holy Spirit to do the heavy lifting, let's be faithful in asking or saying the things God puts on our hearts in those moments of vulnerability. Let's speak the truth wrapped in a thick cloud of love to the people for whom we have the heaviest of hearts.

TO THOSE WHO ARE PROGRESSIVE CHRISTIANS:

I understand why you landed where you did. I really do. I almost landed there myself. But, my beloved friend, it's time to come home. The sun is going down. A warm supper is on the table and the One whom you are subconsciously seeking in all the things you are exploring is sitting down to eat. He's looking around the table at his friends who trusted and believed his words. Where are you? You were once inside his home and enjoyed all that is his, but you were enticed outside by the lies of an accuser who used God's gifts to you—a heart of compassion, a curious mind, a desire to help the marginalized—to turn you against God.

Come back inside. Dine with the King who knows your name, who formed you, shaped you, and allowed every ounce of his blood to be spilled for you. I know there are catchy phrases like "cosmic child abuse" coming to your mind right now, but that's one of the lies used against you. Twisty phrases have been designed to make the cross of Christ look weird and unnecessary (e.g., "God sacrificed himself to save us from… himself?"). Don't believe those words. He died because he loves you. Trust in the simplicity of that and come back inside. Before the sun sets, please come back home.

BEFORE THE SUN SETS, PLEASE COME BACK HOME.

My own footprints are still fresh in the damp night grass from when I left and came back. This was the realization I experienced when I came home, and these are the words I long to hear you say too:

"I have come home at last! This is my real country! I belong here. This is the land I have been looking for all my life, though I never knew it till now. The reason why we loved the old Narnia is that it sometimes looked a little like this. Bree-hee-hee! Come further up, come further in!"
—C. S. Lewis, *The Last Battle*

ACKNOWLEDGEMENTS

I want to thank some people in my life who helped make this book a reality. Firstly, I want to thank Jesus for walking with me every step of the way. What an amazing journey this has been! On the mountains and in the valleys, you were with me. Thank you for never letting go.

I also want to thank my lovely wife, Summer, for listening to me talk at length about this story and about writing and about this book as well as other books rumbling around in my mind: I really appreciate you never making me feel silly for the creative visions God continually gives to me. I'm so glad God matched me with another dreamer! Living up in the clouds with you has been the joy of my life.

I also want to thank my parents for believing in every single project I've ever worked on in my life. You not only believed in me; you've been genuinely interested in whatever my brain conjures up, supportive when things didn't work out, and visibly proud of me when things went well. Thank you for that, and also thank you for taking me to church as often as you did. You gave me the right foundation to not only kick off against when I launched into my own chapter of our faith, but also something solid to return to when I was done wandering. God answered your prayers to keep me close to him all those years I was deconstructing.

I want to thank the leaders at my church (specifically Bobby, Doug, JP, Mike and Michelle, and all the elders): you have not only discipled me and changed the trajectory of my life and my family's lives, but you've also given me the time and space to develop my gifts and to chase down dreams that God has given me. You laid hands on me and prayed over me when I was weak, and you built me back up and encouraged me. In prayer you laid hands on my wife and asked for her healing. You walked us through deliverance and helped us live free! Thank you does not quite cover it! Also, thanks to my friend in heaven, Josh Patrick. Thank you for hearing my story and taking a chance on me at Harpeth. That completely changed my life.

Huge thanks to Bobby, Jason, Daniel, and Jean at Renew.org. You guys also fit into the category as my church. You've given me such freedom in pursuing the creative ventures God has placed on my heart. Thank you for giving me the outlet to share my story! Thank you to Chad and Bryana at YouPublish for creating a sick book cover.

Thanks to my best friend, Matt, for all the positive conversations we've had about de/reconstructing. You were there when most of this stuff was happening!

ACKNOWLEDGEMENTS

And thanks to you, the reader. Hearing from many of you that you resonated with my story has been one of the high points of my life. I wondered if there were people like me, but I felt I might be alone. It fills me with tons of joy to know there were people out there dealing with the same things I was. And what a relief to know that a lot of you that wandered came back to the historic faith. I may never meet you this side of heaven, but when we're there…come find me. We'll have a lot of catching up to do.

ABOUT THE AUTHOR

Dave Stovall is an author, speaker, singer/songwriter, worship minister at Harpeth Christian Church in Franklin, TN, music producer, musician, and videographer. He is the lead singer of Renew Creative and Wavorly and a former bass player for Audio Adrenaline. He is married to a beautiful sunflower of a girl named Summer and they have three kids together: Bear, Byrdie, and Basil. They live happily in the quiet country-land of Primm Springs, TN, where they take care of their little chaotic, wannabe farm: Sonny, Mimi, and Fig (dogs); Miss Olivia, Catch, Sootie, Stacy, Marble, Faerie, and Glittersparkles (chickens); and Cookie and Lucky (cats).